YOUR JOB AND HOW TECHNOLOGY WILL CHANGE IT

YOUR JOB AND HOW TECHNOLOGY WILL CHANGE IT:

Surviving & Succeeding
in the New Work World

Richard Lieberman

2000

First edition published in 2015 by Management Books 2000 Ltd
This new edition published in 2015 by Management Books 2000 Ltd
36 Western Road
Oxford OXI 4LG
Tel. 0044 (0) 1865 600738
Email: info@mb2000.com
Web: www.mb2000.com

British Library Cataloguing in Publication is available

ISBN 9781852527495

To Tina, Todd, and Claire, and to the memory of my parents

"Work could cure almost anything.
I believed that then, and I believe it now."

– Ernest Hemingway,
A Moveable Feast

TABLE OF CONTENTS

Introduction

I am sitting in an outdoor coffee shop in a small Florida town, wearing shorts and a tee shirt, writing this book. If I need research material, I have immediate access to a previously unimaginable wealth of books, articles, and studies on my iPad. On my Kindle, I can review the dozens of research books that I have notated for this project. If I want to interview someone, I can instantly text, email, or call anyone in the world on my smartphone. I am using that phone to dictate this book, and my voice travels to a "cloud," which my secretary in Chicago may access at any time to type up my words.

At a table across from me a grizzled guy is smoking a cigarette, using a computer and a cellphone. He looks up at me and says, "Good place to work."

I respond, "Great place to work." I ask him, "Are you working now?"

"Yes."

I try to guess what his job is, but I cannot do so with any level of confidence because he could be doing any number of jobs. In a few years' time, the fellow sitting across from me could be doing any type of work that exists in the world. He could be a supply chain manager for a multinational corporation dealing with a supplier in South Korea about the dimensions of a part for a brake system in a truck manufactured in Ireland. He could be an Ivy League college professor preparing a video lecture on Jane Austen's final novel that will be streamed to 125,000 English literature college students around the globe. He could be a prominent heart surgeon prepping for surgery, which he will perform on a computer from his condo around the corner on a patient in Naples, Italy. He could be a car mechanic providing instructions on his laptop to a robot replacing an exhaust pipe in a repair shop located 50 miles away.

In recent years there have been many books and articles by experts about how technology will change the world. These experts talk about the macroeconomic ramifications of technological change and how it will create or destroy jobs. They discuss the effect on business, science, healthcare, education, and personal privacy. They address the specific technology itself—the new gadgets and tools. But it seems that no one is really examining what the technological revolution will mean to you, to your job, and to your day-to-day life. How will it affect you personally? Will your life change? How will technological change affect us at the most personal level: what we do every day, every hour, where and how we work and live. The lyrics from a 1960's song may resonate with you as you look at the changes in the world around you today: "There's something happening here. What it is ain't exactly clear."[1] At your workplace and in your personal life, people appear to be living and working just as they always have—a home in the suburbs, commute to a work place where they labor for eight or nine hours, and then travel home. But something is different now; you just can't quite put your finger on what it is.

Recently I began telling a friend, who is in his mid-60's and head of sales for a large corporation, about my book project. Once he got the drift of what I was saying, he interrupted me, declaring, "I hate email and all this technology. I come into the office every day, and I have to respond to all these emails. If I don't, people get upset. I don't even want to understand or try to understand how to work these damn technology tools. I despise them." As I researched and conducted interviews for this book, I realized that his sentiments were simply an honest reflection of the feelings of millions of workers, most of

1   Stephen Stills, "For What It's Worth," 1967, ATCO

whom are over 40. They are fearful of technology, that it will hurt, not help, them in their work and personal life. The mainstream media feeds their negative views of technological change. There is article after article about how people are distracted by their mobile devices, unable to productively work when they multi-task, have lost their ability to have normal social interactions because of texting, have seen their privacy disappear, and on and on and on. Even articles extolling technological advances temper it with handwringing about adverse ramifications. Of course the mainstream media has good reason to be upset about technology, as it is effectively destroying the print media business (newspapers, magazines, and books). Craigslist and other online advertising companies have sucked the classified advertising revenues from newspapers and magazines, sending many of them into bankruptcy. It is no wonder that, at times, the media deprecates technological advances.

In this book, I am not going to discuss whether these changes are good or bad. They are coming regardless of any positive or negative effects. Bemoaning new technology is very much like those people who said passenger airplanes were terrible because they did not provide the comfort, leisure, and sociability of a long train trip. They may have been right, but they completely missed the significance of what was happening. Today, those who complain about technological change in their work life are doing themselves an enormous disservice. They are simply finding an excuse to ignore what is occurring and failing to prepare for the fast-approaching new work world.

I probably would have had the same attitude about technology and its effect on work if not for a series of events that changed my perspective. As a baby-boomer, I followed a traditional, professional career path. I became a partner in a large law firm, and by the early

2000's I was set in the way I performed my job and lived my life. Every day I would take the train to my office in downtown Chicago, where I would talk to clients on the telephone, attend meetings, prepare letters and legal briefs, and appear before judges in court. If there was a meeting with an out-of-town client, I would travel. Over the years, I accumulated a great deal of expertise in the specialized areas of employment and intellectual property law. I knew exactly what I was doing and where everything was. Our filing systems were precise and accurate, and I could find whatever documents or briefs I needed from our extensive files. I never questioned that I would continue to work this way for the rest of my career. However, in 2005, my law firm asked me to move to Los Angeles to open a new office for the firm. With great trepidation, I accepted. Because much of my practice was on the East Coast and in the Midwest, I commuted back and forth between LA and Chicago. At the beginning of this process, I continually sent dozens of boxes of documents back and forth between the two cities. I fretted about having immediate access to all my files, the lifeblood of a lawyer's work. I also worried about the ability of clients to instantly reach me by phone, extremely anxious about not being permanently based in my office in Chicago. Could I perform my job efficiently? Would my clients leave? Would I exhaust myself by constantly moving between two places?

That a lawyer could work entirely without paper, an office, colleagues down the hall, or an infrastructure of administrative support in close physical proximity was a realization that came to me gradually over several years. As I moved back and forth between LA and Chicago, it slowly dawned upon me that clients, colleagues, adversaries, and judges did not really care where I was, nor did they even care to know. I slowly began setting up virtual files for my legal work and accessing those files on my laptop, and then on my smartphone and tablet. After a few years, all of my files—every single document

I worked with—were instantaneously available to me wherever I was. After the 2007 recession, clients wishing to save money cut back on travel, so my face-to-face meetings with out-of-town client diminished. Many clients who were in the same city as me decided that it was more efficient and time-saving to communicate by email rather than having in-person conversations. My work day began to shift outside of traditional hours. When I received a brief from the opposition in an important lawsuit late on the Friday afternoon of the Easter weekend, I decided that it would serve our client's interest to submit our reply brief so that the judge could see it when he arrived in his chambers on Monday morning. Late on Friday afternoon, my team of four lawyers, each working at home in a different geographical location around the country, researched and wrote a highly complex legal brief regarding Constitutional issues. We completed our work late on Sunday night and submitted it through the federal court electronic filing system to the court in Pennsylvania so that the judge had it on his desk (or his desktop computer) when he walked into his office on Monday morning. Throughout our work that weekend, we did not use paper or law books, did not go to an office or library, did not see one another, and did not use a secretary, messengers, or any office infrastructure. We worked at home, shared the Easter holiday with our families, and completed the project over a holiday weekend, which we probably could not have done even a few years before.

What finally dawned on me was that my job as a lawyer had been utterly transformed. Here I was, a middle-aged man, set in his ways, forced by circumstances to completely change the way he worked. As I began working in this new way, I began to see that it was far more efficient, faster, cheaper, and better than the old way. I began to consider the following idea: if the technology that allowed me to work in this new way continued to improve, it would change the entire legal industry. And it struck me that individuals who failed to adapt or resisted these changes would be in trouble; that is, the professionals in my industry would have to learn to work virtually or become obsolete and unemployed. If this was the case for lawyers, I reasoned, certainly it would be the same for accountants, consultants, and others providing intellectual services. As I began researching and conducting interviews for this book and looking at jobs in other industries—including healthcare, teaching, retail, and manufacturing—I began to see that the technological revolution was going to change every industry, every profession, every job, and every person's life. I realized that we are on the brink of a seismic change in the way all work is performed.

To research this book, I interviewed many baby-boomer corporate leaders and executives. In direct contradiction to my conclusions that we will experience a major change in the way people work, almost all of the leaders told me that they foresaw no significant changes in the work world. They viewed work technology as "tools" to help employees perform their traditional jobs and believed that the conventional 19th/20th century office workplace is necessary for employees to collaborate, be assessed by their supervisors, and have access to all the physical objects—documents, files, telephones, computers, and desks—that they need to perform their work. In their view, to efficiently do a job, people need to report to work at a certain time and leave work at a certain time, have face-to-face interactions with co-workers for collaboration, and need to meet with bosses so their strengths and weaknesses can be judged based on their social skills and their performance can be judged using objective and subjective measures. It was difficult for me to find any high-level executives in major corporations who felt there was an impending fundamental change in the nature of jobs and work. They all believed that the traditional work model would remain unchanged.

But when I spoke to younger employees at these companies, they saw the work world in a different way. Many were already redefining their jobs, in some instances under the radar of their bosses. They worked different hours, worked remotely, and used state-of-the-art software and hardware that was not available from their company. Many expressed frustration with the constraints imposed upon them by old-fashioned work rules and their companies' clumsy enterprise software. They believe that change is coming to the work world, and they are already working in different ways than their older colleagues. One informal survey that I conducted showed almost a direct age correlation in the use of paper documents—the younger the employee, the less likely they were to use paper. Individuals 40 and above tended to work predominantly with paper files, but as I talked to people going down the age spectrum, the percentages dropped almost in complete correlation to their age. For the young professionals two or three years out of school, most of them said that 85% of their work was done on computer, smartphone, or tablet screens, and it would have been 100% if not for the fact that the available software did not permit them to manipulate some content to achieve their purposes, so they were forced to use the actual documents to achieve their desired result. These workers are already working in a paperless, virtual work world, and have disdain for the old ways. One brilliant young woman said, "I don't understand why our company's software does not permit a single virtual document to be available to the entire team, with everyone's notations and observations on a single document. As it is now, one document is in the computer system in dozens of formats and permutations. And the enterprise software does not permit a sensible, orderly, and easy to access filing system. If anything, the software seems to be designed to make access, organization, and filing as cumbersome and inefficient as possible." When I mentioned these observations to more senior individuals in the company, they scratched their heads. I've talked to some young employees who avoid the company enterprise software and instead use commercially-available software so that they can more easily access and use their data and documents on their tablets.

These young professionals also resent the rules of their bosses who expect to see them in the office at a particular time to print out memos, place them on the bosses' desk, and wait for an office meeting to discuss them. One individual said, "I spent Friday through Sunday working on a massive project. Why do I have to make a long commute to be in the office on Monday morning at 9:00 to put a hard copy on the boss' desk and then wait for his handwritten comments to come back to me down the hallway? It is a waste of time." It appears that the older and younger employees of the same organization are in different work worlds, and there is a silent generation gap. The older employees continue to work in the same traditional way, while the younger employees are embracing the technology to allow them to work virtually and more efficiently.

When I began working on this book, I thought the big story was about how technology was changing work and how people performed their jobs, but I eventually realized that was not it. It is the employees themselves, particularly young employees, who are changing their jobs by *collaborating* with new technology to be more productive. Technology is not changing work; rather, innovative and resourceful workers are changing work. Over my years as an employment lawyer, I became an expert in analyzing jobs: breaking down job duties into their specific components and documenting what an individual did from the moment they started their work day to its very last moment. When I started my career in the 1970's, my cases usually involved traditional manufacturing and white-collar, salaried jobs. A job was pretty much the same regardless of the individual performing it; that is, an employee on the assembly line making a particular auto part did the same thing as her co-worker on the line. The white-collar employee, under close supervision of a boss, did the same work as her colleagues. The written job description accurately described the job as it was actually performed. However, in the 1980's, things began to change. With layoffs, leaner workforces, and less supervision, I observed that employees were modifying their jobs. Two individuals working in a retail clothes store selling the same product during the same working hours could be performing different jobs. One employee might spend the day organizing the stock and answering customer questions, while the other employee might serve as a fashion consultant, intuitively knowing what clothes to suggest to the customer and how to dress them. I saw real differences in the way people performed the same job in every category of employment; while two people might hold a job with identical pay and job descriptions, these two individuals were spending their work days doing very different tasks, effectively designing their own jobs. In recent years, with the new technologies, even the most traditional jobs are as much influenced by the employees' ingenuity and intelligence as they are by the job description. With fewer supervisors and leaner workforces, good employees improvise to most efficiently and effectively accomplish the job tasks. The new technology gives them more discretion to mold their jobs, and it is the young people who are most adept at using technology to work most efficiently.

I recently spent the day in an underground coal mine where miners have historically performed rote manual labor. In the past, the coal miners were interchangeable, since they performed nearly identical functions and duties. Today, a coal miner uses advanced technology. If you observe the mining of coal today, you will see a small group of individuals, some operating computer control devices, others observing or directing machinery as it scrapes coal off the walls of the mine. No employee is static, and no one is repeating any task. Each individual is self-directed and collaborates with their co-workers through state-of-the-art technology. I could see that the coal miners were determining what needed to be done in a cooperative process between man and technology.

A recent college graduate employed in a sales and marketing job for a recruiting company received several months' training at its California headquarters office, but when I interviewed her she worked alone, in a small office, 1500 miles from her colleagues. Each day she has a short video (Skype) meeting with her manager. Other than that, she is on her own. Most of her communications with her boss are via text. She rarely uses email or the telephone. Prospective and current clients hold their meetings with her on GoToMeeting, a computer video site. Only about 10% of her client meetings are in person, typically three or four times a year. Each day she decides what she will do, how she will do it, and the priority of work tasks. Her job is to assist clients in identifying job candidates using sophisticated social networking technology; however, the way she approaches her tasks and duties are very much left to her. She is defining the job and the way she does it. She does not feel like she is isolated or cut off because the technological tools put her in constant communication with clients, colleagues, and supervisors. Her supervisor knows what she is accomplishing because she can objectively monitor her productivity and results. She says her biggest challenge is to take enough work breaks to have a good and healthy lifestyle. "It is easy to overwork when I am doing this," she told me.

The new technology, coupled with the individuality of workers, particularly younger people, is creating new type of work where individuals performing jobs are molding the jobs themselves. While their employers may set the broad goals and objectives, these individuals are determining how their jobs can best be performed. They are determining where, when, and how to do the work, and, with the ongoing availability of new technology, they will create, refine, and then re-create the same job so that jobs will no longer be static. Indeed, unless the job is continually changed by the worker, that worker will become inefficient compared to others doing the same job.

This is happening right now, particularly with workers born after 1987. For the most part, management is only partially cognizant of what is occurring. They either don't see it, or, in all too many cases, try to tell younger workers to work the old-fashioned way. But in the next few years, what is quietly occurring now will become the norm.

The development of new, super-robust technologies will eliminate the need for a central workplace where employees must go each day. Instead, physical files will be virtual, colleagues will be located all around the world, and bosses will not need to directly observe and monitor their employees. The accepted wisdom that employees' job performance can only be assessed by personally observing them in an office is similar to the now-discredited approach in professional baseball where ballplayers were selected by looking at their physical appearance and making subjective judgments as to the way they swung or ran, or via unsubstantiated statistical information. These measures were shown to be inaccurate measures of success by a new breed of statistical experts who used objective, verified data such as on-base percentage. It didn't really matter if a scout said that the player looked great or had a terrific swing: it was the objective statistical data that mattered.[2] We will see this in the work world as

2   Michael Lewis, *Money Ball: The Art of Winning an Unfair Game* (W.W. Norton & Company, Inc., 2003).

technology makes work performance so transparent so that work can be readily measured by efficiency, timeliness, quantity of production, and any number of objective indicators. How employees look, who they schmooze with, and whether they are good-looking Caucasian males from an Ivy League school or overweight, disabled females from Oklahoma will not matter one whit. In the new technologically-based work world, what will count is objectively measured job performance.

While for the last several decades we have been the beneficiaries of extraordinary technological advances providing powerful tools to help people perform their jobs, technology has not fundamentally changed the way people work. For the most part we still commute to a central workplace, work fixed hours at a desk or counter or machine, and then go home at the end of the workday. Physicians still examine their patients in an office or hospital. Teachers still stand in the front of the classroom using an old-fashioned chalkboard to impart knowledge to their students. Factory workers still stand at a stationary position in a workspace. Accountants continue to sit at a desk doing their work, albeit on a computer screen rather than with paper spreadsheets. So what is it about this particular moment in time that is different? Why are we at a transition point in the way we work?

A large part of the catalyst for change is an explosive increase in computer power, now expanding so rapidly that it will soon provide a foundation for new work technology. Moore's Law, which states that computer power doubles every few years, is much like compound interest. At first the accumulation of capital from the interest seems small, but as the interest and principal continues to compound over the years, the imperceptible growth at the beginning reaches a point in time where the modest amount of money turns into enormous wealth. Think of it in this way: if you had $5,000, which doubled in several years, that would be a wonderful gain, but you would not be rich and powerful. However, if that doubling continued for decades, the amounts become large, and wealth and power would be created. This is where we are now with computer power. Ray Kurzweil, an inventor and futurist, documents how the early increases in technology power such as chip speed, memory storage, and Internet speed, were reflected by modest growth on a curve. But at this point in time, each cycle of doubling results in a tremendous leap in computer power. In the 20th century, what was equivalent to 20 years of technological progress, in the year 2000 would be 14 years of progress, and for the 21st century, it will be a thousand times greater than what was achieved in the 20th century.[3] By the second decade of the 21st century, the growth curve will be almost straight up. We are now nearing a point in time where the power of computer chips, sensors, Internet broadband, and cloud storage will create a platform for an incredibly robust work technology.

As a result, bold predictions of futurists like Kurzweil less than a decade ago have already been surpassed by technological advances that seemed like science fiction then. For example, until recently, it was believed that the ability of a robot to recognize patterns in a room and then navigate through it without bumping into anything would be unattainable in our lifetime. Scientists believed that the human ability to look at objects and images and then make judgments as how to maneuver and manipulate them was so incredibly complex that technology was not even close to designing a robot that could do that. The lowest insect had better processing skills and common sense than a robot because it could dodge and weave around corners to avoid bumping into things, whereas a robot, unless

3   Ray Kurzweil, *The Singularity Is Near: When Humans Transcend Biology* (Penguin Books, 2005), 56-84.

specifically programmed, could not do the same. Consequently, robots would be limited in their work usage because they were restricted in pattern recognition and common sense.[4] But we are now at the tipping point, where robots with supersonic chips, sensors with optical scanners, and limitless access to information from clouds and memory storage will soon have the ability to see, analyze, and process and then put into action extraordinarily complex movement and activities beyond what was believed possible a few years ago.[5]

C & S, a large grocery wholesaler, traditionally used a half million square foot warehouse where hundreds of employees drove pallets, jacks, and forklifts to move thousands of items of stock on and off shelves to supply grocery stores. Its "new warehouse" near New York City is only 30,000 sq ft and is staffed by 168 "rover" robots that look like Go Karts and can move at 25 mph. Each robot is wirelessly connected to a single computer, which provides instruction as to when and which products to move from place to place. On command, the robots speed to the appropriate location, where, using a ten-foot-tall arm that has the dexterity of a human's, they lift, twist, and turn the cases to fit into the proper locations. A bird's eye view of the warehouse shows robots zooming around, retrieving and packing goods for shipment. Software algorithms determine the priority and method for the robots to do their work. Consequently, there is no traffic jam as the robots move stock through the warehouse like digital bits being processed by a computer.[6]

Robots now have better dexterity and accuracy than a human hand, permitting doctors to partner with robots to perform surgery. For

4   Michio Kaku, *Physics of the Future: How Science Will Shape Human Destiny and Our Daily Lives by the Year 2100* (Doubleday, 2011), 67-68.

5   "Modest Debut of Atlas May Foreshadow Age of 'Robo Sapiens'," *New York Times*, 11 July 2013.

6   "Skilled Work, Without the Worker," *New York Times*, 18 August 2012.

open heart surgery, robots can make small incisions and work within the body in a far less invasive manner than a human hand. In the near future, it will not be necessary for the surgeon to be in the same room as the patient, as the surgery will be performed remotely. Consequently, highly specialized microscopic surgery on blood vessels, nerve fibers, and tissues will be available to patients regardless of geographical location. Patient will have access to the most appropriate doctor for their condition regardless of location.[7]

Also, it seemed unimaginable that a car could operate in real traffic without a driver during our lifetime. But Google has already done it, modifying a car so that it can drive without human involvement. These cars are use information from Google Maps, video, radar, and light detection to analyze what is around them and where they are. In the near future, we will be safer on the road if we let the car drive itself.[8]

Likewise, voice recognition software has long been an imperfect technology. Experts did not see it becoming a mainstream technology for a long time, perhaps decades. The notion that one could ask a smartphone for the closest Thai restaurant, research assistance, or translation to another language and immediately receive accurate information seemed far off even a few years ago, but now it is a basic feature on smartphones.[9]

Another technology that will change jobs is 3D printing. When I ask people if they know what 3D printing is, most either don't know or

---

7   Kaku, 82; Farhad Manjoo, "Will Robots Steal Your Job," Slate.com, (2011); Eric Topol, *The Creative Destruction of Medicine* (Basic Books, 2011), 192-193; Michael Saylor, *The Mobile Wave: How Mobile Intelligence Will Change Everything* (Persell Books/Vanguard Press, 2012), 158-160.

8   Erik Brynjolfsson and Andrew McAfee, *Race Against the Machine* (Digital Frontier Press, 2011), 14.

9   Ibid., 14, 15.

believe it has something to do with printing paper with 3D images. Actually, it is a new method for manufacturing. Visualize your home computer with an image on the screen; you push the "print" button and the document comes out of your printer. In the near future, imagine that the carburetor on your car is worn out. You may put a 3 dimensional image of the carburetor of a 2007 Dodge on your screen and push the "print" button, which activates a small machine, resembling a paper printer, located in your garage. Within the machine is a basin of liquid resin and a laser. The machine, responding to your computer instructions, begins tracing patterns in the resin in the precise shape of the carburetor. The liquid hardens, and the carburetor is formed at the base of the machine out of the liquid. You remove it, take it over to your Dodge, pull out the defective unit, and connect the new carburetor. It works perfectly. But you are a dedicated car hobbyist, so you would like to modify the carburetor so that it is supercharged. You go back to your computer, pull up the image of the standard carburetor, and begin to modify it on the screen to incorporate the functions you want. When you're satisfied, you push the button again, and the machine prints a custom carburetor. You install it in your car and drive it, but you are not completely satisfied with the results. You return to your computer, make some additional modifications, and this time it does precisely what you want. Your costs are less than ten dollars for the resin and the patented carburetor design.[10]

Here is how the 3D process works. It uses a Computer Assisted Design (CAD) program, which is a series of geometric equations that can instruct a machine to reproduce the designed object in any size and in any medium (i.e. plastic, metal, cloth, or tissue). Most 3D printing machines use additive technology; that is, they

10   Chris Anderson, *Makers: The New Industrial Revolution* (Crown Business, 2012), 81-83.

build the product layer by layer from a liquid, such as resin. Some machines use subtractive technology, using an old-fashioned drill, saws, or cutters to make products from plastic, wood, metal, paper, or fabric. Some use quilters and embroidering machines for fabrics, or powerful lasers can cut patterns of great complexity into sheets of whatever materials you wish, producing objects as large as an airplane fuselage. The computer program itself can also act as a scanner, but rather than scanning a picture, they scan an existing object using a special camera to image the object from all sides. The scanner converts the object into a 3D image on your computer, which you can modify if you wish, and then push a button to print the product.[11]

3D printing technology is already being used in jewelry, footwear, industrial design, architecture, engineering, instruction, automotive, aerospace, dental, medical, education, geographic information systems, civil engineering, and more.[12] It is in its early stages, but it will become mainstream in the manufacturing sector. While you may think that manufacturing is now irrelevant to work in the US, it is still an enormous source of jobs—in 2012, 12 million Americans were employed in manufacturing jobs, with manufacturing contributing 1.87 trillion to the economy, or 12% of GDP.[13]

Consequently, it should not be surprising that new technology is becoming the centerpiece of manufacturing production. There are many examples. A company in San Francisco is preparing to go to market with artificial replacement limbs (arms and legs)

---

11 Anderson, 89-92; Shawn Wallace, "Maker Faire New York," *MAKE* (26 September 2012); Sarah Rich and Alex Madrigal, "A Tiny Balloon Factory, Small-Batch Whiskey, and 3D Printing: A Dispatch from the Future of Manufacturing," *The Atlantic*, 26 September 2012.
12 "3D Printing," Wikipedia.
13 Bureau of Economic Analysis, Industry Economic Accounts (2011); Bureau of Labor Statistics (2012).

using 3D printers. They will be completely customized for the individual patient, far less expensive than the off-the-shelf, ill-fitting artificial limbs currently available. Currently, the cost of a high quality replacement limb is in the six figure range, whereas the superior 3D limbs will cost between $5,000 and $10,000 and will be instantaneously available, as opposed to waiting for weeks or months for delivery.[14] In the construction industry, a University of Southern California professor has developed a large 3D printer that will build a wall of a house within 24 hours, reducing the cost of building by 20%. There is also a new robotic building system that can create stone-like structures for full-sized sandstone buildings, which the architect will design using a CAD program and then push a button to "print" the building.[15] There are already 3D manufacturing factories in operation—essentially factories in a cloud. These web-based service bureaus use digital fabrication tools to manufacture designs from around the world. Ponoko, based in New Zealand, provides a service where the customer makes the design on her own desktop and uploads the file to the Ponoko website, where Ponoko examines the file with their software to ascertain whether it's producible and guides the customer through choices as to how to make it. The product may be laser cut from plastic, wood, or aluminum; molded from a liquid resin; or a 3D printer can produce a ring, table, ceramics, or even circuit boards.[16]

In addition to making products customized and immediately available to the consumer, 3D technology can also make them safer. While the technology will permit someone to print a handgun, the availability of cheap and effective sensors could allow the weapons to sound an alert when it is within 1,000 feet of a school or public place.

14   Brad Hart, "Will 3D Printing Change the World?," *Forbes*, 6 March 2012.
15   Marcel Bullinga, "Welcome to the Future Cloud," (Future Tech 2012), Loc. 4465.
16   Anderson, 213-214.

Introduction

"General purpose technologies" is the term economists have given to unique technological breakthroughs that completely change the way people live and work. They include the internal combustion engine, electricity, and steam power. These general purpose technologies result in innovation to business practices and processes, and enormous productivity gains for the worldwide economy. They are game changers.[17]

Computers have already become the general purpose technologies of our time, resulting in changes in virtually every area of business and industry. For example, computerized customer relations management systems permit a corporation to monitor and control worldwide operations and access and analyze relevant information in conducting its business.[18]

The impending convergence of an unprecedented powerful infrastructure of chips, cloud and sensors will result in new general purpose technologies that will lead to business processes which will fundamentally change the way we work. On a macroeconomic scale, we will see the methods and means of manufacturing change, driven by far more efficient, cost-saving technology. Super-robust technology will completely alter the healthcare, education, and service professions, along with every single occupation and job in the world. It is already happening, but the exponential growth of the power of technology, now reaching a tipping point, is about to bring a tidal wave of change to the work world. What we do in our jobs, where we live and work, and how we play will all be different. We are on the cusp of a new working world comparable to the passage from the agricultural to the industrial age. In the new work world, while many traditional jobs will remain in a virtual form, entirely new jobs will also be created, while other jobs will be eliminated completely.

17   Brynjolfsson and McAfee, 20.
18   Ibid., 20, 21.

Whether there will be an overall increase or decrease in jobs in the US or world job market is impossible to predict, and whether there will be a short-term decrease followed by a long-term increase in employment is unknowable. Some economists believe that the lingering unemployment following the 2007 recession was due, in part, to companies determining that they could permanently replace laid-off employees with technology. Data shows that many jobs requiring technological skills remain unfilled, while employees with industrial jobs skills remain unemployed. But whether these changes will increase or decrease overall employment is not the subject of this book. Rather, the premise is that the future virtual work world will create job opportunities for those who can use technology as an integral part of their job. New opportunities will exist in every industry and job, but those who continue to work in the traditional ways, believing the technology is not a fundamental component of their job, will be underemployed or jobless.

It is the younger workers, the digital natives who were born after 1987, who will lead the way, aggressively adopting new work technologies so they can perform more efficiently and economically. Workers who fail to change and adapt will be vulnerable because the marketplace will reward those individuals who collaborate with the new technology. With much more robust work technology, workers will be empowered to change, define, and structure the nature of their jobs in a way they never could in the past. Rather than the employer controlling the job by defining the precise duties and dictating where and when the employee works, in the near future, the employees will effectively make those decisions. In doing so, the workers themselves will change the basic nature of work. This is where the revolution will occur. In the final analysis, the nature of work will change not because management decides that it is a good idea, but because the economic efficiencies will be superior to traditional work methods. In the end, competition will drive the change, as the organizations and workers who adopt the newest technology will succeed in the marketplace.

This will happen soon; in fact, it is happening already. I learned to work in a new way because circumstances forced me to do so. If I had remained in my comfortable office in Chicago, I would have continued, like so many of my colleagues in my age group, to do my job in the same way until such time as my way of doing things became too expensive and inefficient for clients to pay for. The marketplace has always required that the job be done as efficiently and as cheaply as possible. The extraordinary technology that will be increasingly available in the next few years will create a platform for far more productive companies and workers. Those who can adapt to a virtual work world will be the winners, and those stuck in the past will be in trouble. That's what this book is about, and, most importantly, it is focused on you and what you can do to stay in the game and adapt to a changing work world.

The first chapter of this book will discuss what is this job-changing technology is. The real changes will come as extraordinary new software and hardware is combined with reimagining its uses in the workplace. The new technology will not simply replicate on a screen what workers have traditionally done with paper or machines. Rather, it will provide entirely new methods and means of doing one's job.

Chapter Two delves into why the new technology will change jobs. It asks: what are the drivers to change the existing order of our present work world? The work world has been essentially unchanged since the Industrial Revolution, so why would it change now?

Chapter Three focuses on who will utilize the new work technology, and, as a result, who will hold the jobs and constitute the employment pool.

Chapter Four discuss the actual jobs and how they will look in various industries and professions.

Last, and perhaps most important, Chapter Five addresses how you can get ready for the new work world today. The decline of mid-level white-collar jobs and blue-collar factory jobs in the US has occurred even as more jobs were created in professional, tech, and high level management, food, retail, and personal care service positions. While these categories seem to have nothing in common, they all require what has been deemed "situation adaptability"—the ability to respond to the unique, unexpected circumstances of the moment.[19] Jobs as diverse as running a large department, fixing a computer, or helping a customer in a store to find the appropriate garment all require independent thinking and analysis. The ability to constantly adapt to the work situation, to think flexibly, and to be willing to change with the times that are the basic skills that one needs to compete in the new world. It is the young who are by nature the most open, resilient, and flexible. Unfortunately, many people become more and more rigid in their thinking and actions as they get older. To survive and prosper in this new work world, everyone will have to think and act like a young person. Everyone will have to be open to new ideas and be willing to look at each situation in a fresh way. Chapter Five will provide you with practical steps that you can take to prepare yourself for changes that will occur in your work world.

19 David Autor, "The Polarization of Job Opportunities in the US Labor Market," Center for American Progress and the Hamilton Project, (April 2010).

My intention for this book is to convince you that a work revolution is coming and that you can be among those who are ready for it. We are entering a new work era, providing both great opportunities and pitfalls. The message of this book is that everyone can prosper in this new world.

CHAPTER 1
What Technology Will Change Work?

One major premise of this book is that we are on the verge of achieving an advanced technological foundation that will utterly transform the way we work. So, what is it about the emergent technology that makes it different than it is right now, and why are we on the cusp of a major change in the work world? It is not just one thing. It is not simply evolving mobile devices or new software or hardware. It is really the coming unprecedented levels of computing power and the affordability of technology—a combination of faster computer chips, infinite storage capacity, and ubiquitous sensors, and the way this mighty technology will be reimagined into new ways of performing our jobs.

In the introduction, I talked about Moore's Law, named after Gordon Moore, co-founder of Intel. In the mid 1970's, Moore prophesied that twice as many transistors could be incorporated within an integrated circuit every 24 months. As a result, electrons would travel a smaller distance, making the circuits faster and providing a boost to overall computer power. Moore underestimated the rate of change, because subsequently this doubling rate occurred every 12 months, and it continues to do so. With the chip power doubling each year for the same cost and an increasing number of chips manufactured, there reaches a point in time where there will be a previously-unimaginable amount of computer strength providing a foundation for extraordinary technological innovations. This has profound significance for the world we live in because these chips (technically called "integrated circuits") are the bedrock of virtually all electronic equipment. Chips run everything from home appliances to factory machinery, mobile phones to computers. So if chips become twice as strong every year, the engine that runs our work world is affected in a significant way. Since Moore's Law has been in effect for four decades, what in the early years of the Law was reflected by only incremental gain in computing power is now creating giant gains from year to year. Your cellphone now has more computer capacity than NASA possessed in 1969 when they placed two astronauts on the moon.[20] The Apple iPhone is 400 times more powerful than the first Apple computer from 1976.[21] You want to replace your cellphone or smartphone every two years because the newer models are so hugely superior, largely because of this ongoing increase. You can see Moore's Law happening right in front of you.

We are now entering an explosive stage in the growth of chip capacity, and Moore's Law will continue to have its exponential ramifications into the future. Although at some point scientists will begin having difficulty scaling down circuits to fit on the surface of silicon wafers (chips), researchers are currently inventing new methods and technologies to extend Moore's Law. But even without new inventions, organizations are continuing to double computer power by linking large numbers of processors together in parallel architectures. Essentially, these are parallel computers within the same device. Even today, smartphones contain as many as four processors (cores) which perform tasks at the same time. Another current method of expanding computer power is grid computing, which links different computers together using special software. In other words, computers from all over the world can be connected together to work simultaneously. Consequently, an

20 Kaku, 21.
21 "Wright's Law: A Better Predictor of Technological Progress than Moore's Law," *World Future Society*, (Sept. 2012) Vol. 13, No. 9.

What Technology Will Change Work?

enormous problem can be broken into smaller pieces, distributed across hundreds or thousands of computers to work on the problem simultaneously. This brings unprecedented levels of computer power to a particular problem. The human genome project was advanced by the use of grid computers.[22]

There are also a number of brand new technologies that will extend Moore's Law. One is based on carbon nanotubes: a type of molecule that would replace silicon and create smaller transistors while increasing the speed at which they operate. According to IBM researchers, carbon nanotubes would allow chips to improve by a factor by five or more over the type of silicon devices currently used in chips.[23]

Another promising new technology is the quantum computer, a completely different device from the digital computers that use transistors. Quantum computers make use of something called the quantum mechanical phenomenon, which employs subatomic particles. Quantum computers will process data much faster and thereby will be able to solve problems that classic computers don't have the power to solve. Quantum computing enables computers to do millions of computations at once with a single "qubit." A 250 qubit system has more bits of information than there are atoms in the universe. A traditional bit used in chip-based computing can only value "zero" or "one," while a qubit can have both values at the same time, enabling supersonic computing compared to traditional computing. While there has been work on quantum computing for some time, scientists have recently figured out a way to construct these super-conducting qubits with traditional silicon fabrication

22 Martin Ford, *The Lights in the Tunnel, Accelerating Technology and the Economy of the Future* (Acculant Publishing, 2009), 42.
23 "IBM Reports Nanotube Chip Breakthrough," *New York Times*, 28 October 2012; "Google Buys a Quantum Computer," *New York Times*, 16 May 2013.

techniques.[24] In 2012, IBM scientists announced that they made breakthroughs in quantum computing that put them "on the cusp of building systems that will take computing to a whole new level."[25] As part of their work, IBM researchers have stored and retrieved digital data from an array of only 12 atoms, pushing the boundaries of the magnetic storage of information beyond anything seen before.[26] A few years ago, scientists did not expect to see commercial use of quantum computing for at least a decade, but they underestimated its development progress, for the first such computer will soon be used by major corporations.[27]

Even without any new scientific breakthroughs, the continued doubling of computer power will provide a foundation for software that will change the work world. We are not waiting for a Flash Gordon breakthrough—it is already here.

With cheap, far more powerful chips, desk and laptop computers and tablets will become obsolete. We will be able to wave our finger, and suddenly a visual image will emerge on a wall or in the air, which will be the new computer.[28] The mobile devices such as smartphones and tablets that we currently regard as so revolutionary are simply transitional devices. In the near future, we will be online all the time with ambient devices that are chips imbedded in our clothes, furniture, walls, glasses, fingernails, or anywhere else you can imagine. Mobile will become "me." There will be clouds of information around us anytime, anyplace, anywhere, connecting us to everyone, providing any information we need.[29]

24 Douglas Perry, "IBM Says Practical Quantum Computers are Close," http://www.hardware.com/ibm-qubit-super-computers, 14832.html
25 "Quantum Computer," Wikipedia.
26 "New Storage Device is Very Small at Twelve Atoms," *New York Times*, 12 January 2012.
27 "A Strange Computer Promises Great Speed," *New York Times*, 21 March 2013.
28 Kaku, 32-33.
29 Jeff Jarvis, *Public Parts* (Simon & Schuster, 2011), 151.

The second technological foundation that will change the work world is cloud computing. A cloud is essentially a storage unit (think of a locker at a self-storage place) that retains information that can be accessed anytime and anywhere by the user through the Internet. Technically, the information is stored on a server: a computer that uses software to store information which the user can gain access to over the Internet.[30] At first there was limited ability and great expense to storing information in a cloud, but recently, as large companies began to see the business advantage of unlimited storage, the demand and the availability of cloud computing greatly increased. Grid computing (linking computers), previously discussed, is also being used for cloud storage. This involves a great number of computers, in some cases from different companies or providers, being used on an as-needed basis for additional storage. So if the need increases, a company offering cloud computing services can tap into other computers for storage.[31]

Presently there are enormous computer cloud server "farms" providing cloud services to consumers, who can access them from anywhere in the world. The largest is offered by Amazon (Elastic Computer Cloud), and prices are dropping rapidly. You probably have noticed how Amazon, Apple, and Dropbox offer free storage for your personal data up to a certain point and more storage after that for a fee. Soon, there will be unlimited storage available at very reasonable cost to anyone who wants to rent it.[32]

For companies or individuals who are distrustful of sending their confidential data to a cloud, recent advances in solid state computer memory (flash) will permit immense storage capability in on-site

30 "Server," Tech Terms.com.
31 Ford, 43.
32 Topol, 13-14.

computers at a very inexpensive price. The lightweight storage technology that we currently see in an iPod is about to become vastly more powerful at an extremely cheap price so that individuals and businesses can store their own information on personal storage devices if they wish.[33] There is now a storage unit for about $600 that can contain all of the world's recorded music.[34]

Much like Moore's Law, computer storage capacity (Kryder's Law) doubles every 23 months. So with increased file compression and other advances, ten times as much digital material could be packed into the space now occupied by today's typical MP3 file storage. To put it in more understandable terms, today's 60 gigabyte 15,000 song iPod will be capable of storing 2.4 million songs within the next few years.[35]

The third component creating a foundation for a work revolution is the availability of inexpensive and intelligent sensors. Essentially, a sensor is a device that measures a physical quality such as temperature and converts it into a signal such as 71° F that can be read or converted into some other use. While that seems to be a pretty basic device, digital sensors provide innumerable applications that most people are only dimly aware of. There are now sensors in cars, machines, airplanes, medicine, manufacturing, cameras, robots, and more. The digital image sensor in a camera converts an optical image into an electronic signal. Motion detector sensors (semiconductor sensor detectors) use silicon to detect proton activity that is used in x-rays or particle detectors. Sensors are an important component of robots, detecting and translating what is in the real world to the microcontrollers that operate the robot. In medicine,

---

33   "Tech's New Wave, Driven by Data," *New York Times*, 9 September 2012.
34   Topol, 4.
35   Lee Rainie and Barry Wellman, *Networked, the New Social Operating System* (The MIT Press, 2012), 278.

What Technology Will Change Work?

sensors read vital signs like blood pressure and then convey the information to the appropriate person or machine. The proliferation of sensors resulting from technological advances and their resulting affordability will make them available for an unbelievable array of uses in the immediate future. For example, while optical and radar sensors now are used in cars, new sensors will be rolled out in the next year or so to permit cars to drive themselves, even in heavy traffic, automating freeway driving by keeping the car within its lane and adjusting the car's speed to match the traffic and take over the controls from the driver to prevent an impending accident.[36] Ubiquitous, smaller, and cheaper wireless sensors are the reason why we are starting to see the widespread use of smartphone apps that control the lights in our homes, our security systems, and our front door locks. Sensors will monitor your health, including blood pressure, blood sugar, and heart rate.[37]

There were about ten million wireless sensors in 2009. Within the next few years there will be about 650 million of them, which will provide a sea of sensors in machines, devices, everyday objects, and even in humans. The world will be imbedded with sensors, gathering and transmitting information in real time about everything you can possibly imagine.[38]

In addition to the "compounding interest" growth of chips, clouds, and sensors, Gilder's Law states that Internet connection speeds will double every two years; Nielsen's Law holds that Internet connection speeds will increase 50% every year; and Cooper's Law provides that wireless communications (cellphone, texts, email, tweets, and other data) capability will double every 2.5 years.[39] These technologies

36   "Drivers With Hands Full Get a Backup: The Car," *New York Times*, 12 January 2013.
37   "Smartphones Become Life's Remote Control," *New York Times*, 11 January 2013.
38   Topol, 16.
39   Rainie and Wellman, 278.

have been around for several decades, and they are now approaching the point where they will provide enormous speed, reliability, and capacity.

Recently I returned from LA to my home in Winnetka, Illinois where I discovered that our Internet was not working. I use one of the big telephone providers for my home Internet, but it has operated very poorly since it was installed a number of years ago. Even though I have had many technicians come to my home, it is slow and often out of service. This time the company sent a senior technician who confided in me that their Internet service is flawed and unreliable. He told me that the wiring in the central service area looks like an amateur stuck a bunch of wires together. He managed to get my service up and running, but several days later it went out again. About a week later I traveled up to our summer cottage in Door County, Wisconsin. There we pay a confiscatory sum of $70 per month for Internet service from the only provider available. It usually works extremely well, but upon arriving at the house, I found that the service was down. It took two days for a technician to arrive. He replaced the modem and left, but several hours later we lost Internet again. When I called the company, the representative said it would take three more days to get somebody out. When I protested, they located the same technician, who returned that afternoon. He confided in me that the company no longer provides wireless service because they've had so many problems. They will provide a signal to the house, but the homeowner is on his own in getting a router. He told me that wireless Internet is just not sufficiently developed yet to be reliable, and it was too difficult for their company to deal with all the problems. He eventually managed to get it running, but he told me there was no guarantee that it would be reliable. So, here we are, in the second decade of the 21st century, with major problems in Internet service in the United States. While it can be blindingly fast and reliable in certain places, it is often slow and unreliable in others. Without Internet service that is as reliable as turning on electricity or water, the work world cannot truly change. But given the advances reflected by Gilder's, Nielsen's, and Cooper's Laws, these Internet difficulties will soon be a thing of the past. Consumers are placing a lot of pressure on providers to improve their services. 4G wireless data, which is fast and reliable, will give way to 5G, which has already been developed. And the big providers will soon get their act together on Internet service. When they do, it will provide another fundamental building block for a new work era.

Combining all of this frenzied technological expansion, particularly stupendously fast computer chips with virtually unlimited storage capacity and infinite sensors that can observe, measure, and effectively provide instruction or information regarding everything they record, will soon create an environment that has never before existed in human kind. We are on the verge of having unlimited computer power available to everyone. This is the infrastructure that will transform work for every individual in every job. This technology will not just provide sophisticated work tools–it will redefine the entire workplace. We will not simply be using this technology to do our work; instead, we will be *part* of the technology, completely immersed in it while we live and do our jobs. There will no longer be a separation between us and the technology in the work world; rather, it will be a collaboration between technology and the worker. Because all the information required to perform a job will be instantly available either in a cloud or on a tiny storage device, there will no longer be a need for filing cabinets, desks, storage, offices, paper, or any of the brick and mortar infrastructure that is presently necessary to conduct business. Because of cheap, plentiful sensors, we will be able to monitor, communicate with, and obtain all the relevant information for performing a job. The plant manager based in Omaha will be able to effortlessly observe every aspect of the manufacturing process in his plants in Cork, Ireland, and Singapore through sensors providing images of the factory as well as quality control data and measurements about every minute facet of the manufacturing in those plants. When the plant manager makes decisions, the latest production data projections and all other conceivable information will be instantly available to him in a far more accurate and accessible way than today. This manager, thousands of miles away from his plants, will be far more productive and effective, collaborating with technology to do his job, than he would be if he was physically walking around the factory floor.

So, with this brawny infrastructure of chips, cloud and sensors, coupled with fast, reliable Internet and wireless, what exactly are the technologies that will change work? One is augmented reality. This is adding digital information to the real world around us. Imagine a car mechanic who puts on a pair of glasses and then looks at the engine of a 1998 Jaguar to try to determine why it is knocking. The mechanic sees the specific status of each engine part, including its condition, how it may be defective, where to order a new part if necessary, the price for replacement items, and any other information he might need to analyze the engine. He will also be able to see repair instructions, calculate the labor costs, and determines what competitors are charging for the same job.

We are getting close to widespread availability of augmented reality technology for the work world. For example Google X, the lab where Google develops its inventions, is refining Project Glass, eyeglass frames that can display text, emails, and other information on a miniature screen in front of the wearer's eyes, with the intention of releasing it in the immediate future. With this type of technology, virtual objects and information will be overlaid on a real world image. A tourist visiting Gettysburg would be able to use the glasses to view both the physical battlefield and an overlay with text and even videos describing what happened in that precise locations.[40] An app that is currently available for your smartphone, Layar, performs a similar function. By pointing the smartphone at a ship in the harbor, for instance, a visual flag on the screen provides the name of the ship and other information.[41]

Another technological work world game changer will be virtual communications. While video conferencing has made great strides in the last few years, it will soon appear primitive compared to what is going to happen in the near future. Presently, massive investment is flowing into improving this technology. Microsoft made the largest acquisition in its history last year by paying $8.5 billion for Skype.[42] At the same time Apple is pouring significant resources into its FaceTime app, the results of which we are seeing in easy to use visual communication with iPhone and iPad users. At the same time, there is a rapidly expanding teleconferencing boom as consultants and other businesses facilitate visual meetings between corporate employees around the country and the world.

Where is video conferencing headed? Current teleconferencing technology, where people sit in front of their screen with mediocre visual and audio, unable to see all the participants or observe nuances, will be obsolete. Users will be able to have virtual meetings with one or more colleagues wherever and whenever they want. It will not be necessary to have a computer screen because the images will be projected on any surface from tiny mobile devices or chips.

40 "Despite a Slowdown, Smartphone Advances Are Still Ahead," *New York Times*, 16 September 2012.
41 "Apps That Present Highlights of the World in Front of You," *New York Times*, 20 June 2012.
42 "So Why Did Microsoft Buy Skype?," *Guardian*, 12 May 2011.

In the virtual conference room, all of the participants will be seen in a vivid, three-dimensional surround perspective with perfect sound. There will be the ability to instantaneously access and share documents, video, and any data. The participant will be able to view a running text of the statements made by all the participants like subtitles in a film, with the ability to rewind both text and pictures so that nothing is missed. The meeting will be perpetually recorded and preserved so that participants can review the meeting and search for information in video or text format at their leisure.

Most significantly, these virtual meetings will be better than their real life counterparts. Nothing will be missed because of the clarity, ability to rewind, and other features. Instead of today's logistical hurdles in bringing people together at a single place and time, meetings can be set up instantaneously regardless of where the participants are. The materials needed for review can be accessed in an instant, even if people do not think to get them until the middle of the meeting.

You will not need a laptop or a smartphone to set up one of these meetings, either. Teleconferences may be set up from a chip contained in a pair of glasses or on your fingernail. Think about pointing your finger towards a wall, table, or into the air in order to commence the meeting. Or you may wear special thimbles containing chips and a projector on your fingers to project a screen. Or you may access the screen through chips imbedded in your walls or furniture, turned on like electricity.[43] The MIT Media Lab has already developed a tiny camera and projector worn around your neck that can project an image on anything in front of you.[44]

---

43   Kaku 32.
44   Ibid., 46.

What Technology Will Change Work?

With the infinite capability to pull any information from a cloud, consider your participation in a meeting with 30 people where you can overlay each person's image with relevant biographical data about them. Contrast this to a real life meeting where you are struggling to remember everyone's name. With the new virtual meeting, you will not only have all the information you need about each person, but you will also be able to get their work history and point of view on the topic of discussion. Participants who are speaking in a foreign language will be translated to your own language in audio and text form.

Another likely work-transforming technology is artificial intelligence (AI). Essentially, this involves machines and software that can reason and plan, as well as search, evaluate, analyze, and summarize information. We currently see a whole range of "narrow artificial intelligence" which is software capable of sophisticated analysis, decision making, and reasoning within a relatively narrow field of application. This technology is not really intelligent in the human sense, but rather it is designed to be extremely efficient in performing specific, complex tasks that can be done faster and far more capably than a human. Examples of this are software that pilots or lands airplanes or performs complex financial analysis.[45] This type of artificial intelligence is attracting major commercial investment, creating many new applications. We will see a truly intelligent machine that will be competitive or superior to a human being in its ability to reason and conceive ideas, and it is closer to reality than you may think. IBM's Blue Brain Project, a collaboration between a Swiss university and IBM, attempts to simulate the workings of the human brain. A few years ago Blue Brain beat the world's reigning chess champion, and now it is able to beat humans in the game of Jeopardy.[46]

45   Ford, 241.
46   Ibid., 242.

We are already seeing artificial intelligence combined with search engines, revolutionizing the way professionals and employees can analyze information. One example in the medical field is SimulConsult, a software tool where the doctor enters the patient's symptoms and tests results and the software produces likely diagnoses and the probability of each diagnosis being correct. This tool is designed to collaborate with the physician, providing initial diagnosis based on information in its database compiled from experts in the field, which then prompts the doctor to consider other relevant tests and findings. For example, if the doctor asks about an individual with attention deficit hyperactivity, abnormal lip cardiogram, and physical weakness, the software will inquire about recent salt intake because the artificial intelligence will inform the doctor that sodium can trigger these symptoms.[47]

It is a small step from what artificial intelligence is doing now to locating and summarizing relevant case law for a legal issue and preparing a basic legal brief. Certainly, if AI can now evaluate millions of potential chess moves, it will soon analyze complex legal arguments and provide options and recommendations.[48] We also will have artificial intelligence personal assistants. For example, to make all of the travel arrangements for 50 corporate executives flying to a corporate retreat, artificial intelligence will instantaneously ascertain the appropriate flights, best rates, and transportation to and from the airports in each city.

The New York area airports now have a life-size image of a woman digitally projected on a glass screen that provides information to travelers. A motion sensor detects that an individual is near, prompting a 90 second audio script with baggage claim, taxi stand,

47   "The Doctor of the Future," *Fast Company*, 1 May 2009.
48   Ford, 70-72.

and other basic information. It is easy to see the next improvement in this type of device: the addition of artificial intelligence and sophisticated sensors. Even with narrow artificial intelligence, the device could answer an array of travel questions, and, with an optical sensor, the device could ascertain the category of individual it is dealing with to help to assist in responding to questions. For example, if the optical sensor determined the questioner was a child and the questions indicated that she was lost, the device could call security.

It will be a synthesis of augmented reality, video, and artificial intelligence, enabled by powerful, cheap chips, clouds and sensors, coupled with broadband as reliable as electricity, which will generate the technological foundation for the new work world. With this infrastructure in place, the actual work tools and general purpose technologies will be created. While we currently have many technological tools in rudimentary form, they will be transformed for new and creative uses. Consider tablets, which were around for over 20 years before the arrival of the iPad, as well as the BlackBerry, which predated the iPhone. The iPhone and iPad changed everything. Why? For all their efficiency, BlackBerries were no more than portable e-mail machines with cellphone capability. The original tablets were basic computers that did not work very well. The iPhone and iPad created something entirely new. It was not simply the touch capability, the expanded memory, or their speed, although these are the technical foundation of these products. Rather, it was the interface, which created an entirely different way of playing and working. The user, in effect, enters block pictures on a screen containing music, movies, documents, or search engines, leading to anything and everything. These devices provided far more than ease of use; they created an entirely new thing. Press the screen and the doors open: you are in a weather app that provides more blocks to enter to see the current or future temperature or videos of weather events. Conceptually, it is a brand new way of viewing and manipulating information.

We will soon have many, perhaps infinite, ways of seeing and interacting with content. The present day computer presents documents by replicating on a screen the way they look on paper. In fact, the whole focus of reading documents online is to make them look as much like paper documents as possible. That is why the Kindle has been such an enormous success—the electronic book on a Kindle looks very much like real paper in a real book. But we will soon have the much more powerful technological foundation comprised of chips, cloud and sensors to enable the creation of an entirely new way of looking at content. Nishimura's Law provides that the ability to make better graphic representations, including those that are interactive, doubles every two years, and at the same time, display size doubles every 3.6 years at the same cost. Consequently, representations of people and processes will become much more realistic and dynamic, and visual display will substantially improve.[49] This will provide a foundation for reimagining ways to see and experience content.

New ways of viewing, interfacing, and imagining content is in a way analogous to the movies. When the film industry first started, filmmakers attempted to replicate the theater on film. Films were essentially recorded plays using theatrical acting and stage-bound, slow camera movements. However, soon the visionaries—great artists, directors, and cinematographers—began to entirely reinvent the media using the movement of the cameras, editing, angles, color, light, new ways of writing movie scripts, and more naturalistic acting. They believed a great film was different than a great stage

49   Rainie and Wellman, 278.

What Technology Will Change Work?

play, so they created a new form in order to fulfill their vision. This is what we are going to see with delivery of content. But unlike film, where the creators determine what the film looks like, with the new technology, the user will determine how she wants to view and interact with the content. The technology will provide numerous, perhaps infinite, options to view content. Text, the way we "read" the written word, can be reimagined by the user to best suit her process of assimilating information.

Suppose, for example, that a manager wishes to review the lengthy feasibility study of a new plant in India. The report, prepared by a consultant, is a complex study with statistics, text, video and audio interviews, and pictures of the site. The manager has just been hired by the company and has no prior knowledge of the project. He is at home on a Sunday afternoon and hopes to have some initial conversations with colleagues about it on Monday morning. Sitting on his porch, he uses the small ring on his pinky finger to access a virtual computer that is embedded in a wall in the next room. He prefers to communicate orally, so he tells the computer to enter the company's work site and access the feasibility report. In accordance with his instructions, the software orally communicates with him, asking what he wants from the report. The manager responds that the first thing he would like is a summary that emphasizes the human resources pros and cons of using a local workforce in the plant, as well as a brief summary of the statistics regarding work productivity of that local workforce. He says he would like a verbal report no more than three minutes long. Within seconds he receives a briefing. The artificial intelligence creates an audio report advising that there are other factors that need to be considered regarding the productivity of the plant. The weather conditions are important in this location because there are flooding issues that could affect productivity. The voice further indicates that there are some other intangibles buried in the consultant's report that probably require a more detailed analysis for full understanding. The manager concludes that while this oral summary provided a useful overview, he will need to dig deeper, and the oral presentation is too superficial. So he instructs, "I want to see a visual of the first two sentences of each conceivable factor that might affect worker productivity, in order of importance." Within seconds, text is flashed on the wall, color-coded based on importance. One sentence catches his attention: "Political issues in the local government could result in labor strikes and slowdowns." He asks for the remaining text from the consultant's report on that point, but it is too general and superficial. He determines that he needs much more information. He asks for a virtual keyboard because typing helps him pose the question. He spends 15 minutes preparing a list of questions about the local and political history of strikes, labor unrests, and political issues in this area of India. He submits it, and instantaneously he is shown local newscasts of two violent labor strikes occurring in the area involving multinational companies. Looking at the wall, he skims through the summary of the news articles on the subject. He asks to see the full news articles and any other information regarding the strikes and their underlying issues. Finally satisfied that he is conversant enough to discuss the matter on Monday, he instructs the computer to put together a "content unit" containing everything he deems relevant. He knows that if his colleagues wish to view the content unit, they can do so in the same way he has viewed it, or they can see it in text, audio, or video if they prefer, or project it on a wall, read it on a pair of glasses, hear it in their car as they are travelling, or have it summarized in a way that best suits their approach to assimilating information.

The example I have outlined above is, of course, simply an imagining of this concept. Your conception as to how information can be viewed

What Technology Will Change Work?

and presented is as good as mine. But the big point is we will not be limited to looking at a computer screen or a stack of papers to read a 150-page "document" as the only way to receive information.

If you are reading this thinking that no one really wants this kind of change, you are wrong. We have already seen how more efficient, user friendly, and enjoyable work technology has been adopted even in the face of mighty resistance from corporations. Corporate America embraced the BlackBerry because it provided a simple and secure email phone device, and BlackBerry did a good job of courting corporate IT departments. Apple, which historically ignored the corporate market in favor of consumers, designed the iPhone and iPad for a consumer public who embraced it; within a short period this made Apple the most valuable company in the world. Users of the iPhone, particularly young people, immediately understood that the device was valuable in the work environment because it could do so much more and operated in an entirely different, user friendly way. So they requested and ultimately demanded that their companies allow them to use it in a work setting. At first there was fierce resistance based primarily on corporate inertia and inflexibility, but once companies began to reluctantly allow adaptation, almost overnight the iPhone, iPad, and their clones replaced the BlackBerry in the workplace. The workers who led the revolt for iPhones and iPads used these tools to become more efficient workers.

In the same way, consumers, primarily young people, have already changed and created the way people receive content. A good example is YouTube, which many people mistakenly believe is primarily a music video provider. However, YouTube contains now millions of videos covering every conceivable topic under the sun, from hair care to hydroplaning. Individuals now have their own ongoing YouTube series where they discuss whatever topics are of interest to themselves and their viewers. YouTube is surpassing blogging, which was the first web vehicle to permit interactive text publication of facts and ideas. Now a significant amount of the world's content is provided in video format through YouTube and other providers. This marks a major change in content presentation, and it is only the beginning. As we will discuss in more detail later, new general purpose technologies will make documents, books, and paper wholly obsolete, and screens will no longer simply replicate paper documents; instead, we will access and provide information in entirely new ways.

In this chapter, we have covered the technology that will enable work to change. The question you may be asking is *why* jobs will be performed differently than they are today. After all, we have witnessed significant changes in technology over the past several decades, and yet most jobs look pretty much the same as they did in the past. What is it now that will cause reimagining of how and where work is performed?

What Technology Will Change Work?

CHAPTER 2
Why Technology Will Completely Change the Way We Work

While we have seen tremendous technological changes in our lifetime, we are currently on the cusp of such cheap and powerful computer power, memory and sensors that we will see an extraordinary proliferation of technological work processes, providing such efficiencies and economic savings that corporations and individuals will have no choice but to adopt them. Jobs will become virtual as workers effectively collaborate with technology, and the traditional workplace will disappear. Companies large and small will become truly global as they hire the best employees for the job regardless of their geographical location. People will live in close proximity to their work, and the traditional nine to five workday will disappear as work is performed when appropriate for the project at hand. Workers will collaborate through virtual meetings much like social networking.

Why has this not happened already? There are various reasons. While we have seen extraordinary technological advances, the technology of today is primitive compared to what we are going to see in the immediate future. In addition, there has been inflexibility and limited vision by the leaders of corporate America as to the value of workplace technologies. Enterprise software, which is business software typically used by big and medium-sized companies, has actually lagged behind the most advanced consumer technology because corporate leaders have not seen the business advantages in adopting the best. Corporate executives view work technology as "tools" to help people do their jobs. They do not understand that technology is integral to jobs. Younger workers had to demand adoption of iPhones and iPads in the workplace in the face of resistance by corporate IT departments and their superiors. Every day, young workers bypass the technology available at work by using superior consumer technologies that function more effectively. But even with these changes, for the most part employees continue to work in the traditional way.

Why will this change? The companies and individual workers who adopt the extraordinary new technologies will be able to perform better than their competitors. At the end of the day, the game changer is productivity and economics. Up to this point in time, while work technologies offered great economic advantages, the technologies have not been sufficiently robust to provide a solid foundation for a revolutionary new virtual work world. However in the very near future, convergence of omnipotent chips, clouds and sensors will be the catalyst for a new, all-encompassing virtual work infrastructure. Companies with extensive brick and mortar office buildings and retail outlets will be fatally disadvantaged compared to competitors who conduct business in the virtual world. Those companies that continue to operate and communicate with employees and customers in the old-fashioned way through face-to-face meetings, one-on-one conversations, and emails will be overwhelmed by those companies that enable social network-type environments where they hire the best and brightest talent around the globe who will collaborate in a virtual communication stream with split-second access to all the information they need.

Companies and individuals who are the first to adopt and implement virtual work technologies will defeat their competitors. We have already seen evidence of this. Amazon, recognizing the advantage of online shopping, seized the beachhead early by pouring enormous resources into its website. They waited patiently year after year, losing money, until the business became profitable and eventually began to dominate the retail consumer business. The next wave of technology will create a platform for virtual work environments to create Amazons in every industry, business, and profession.

Since the mid-1990's, there has been a surge in productivity in the United States as a direct result of work-related technology. What is productivity, and why is it important to this discussion? Stated simply, productivity is a measure of the *efficiency* of production. Various factors can increase the productivity of a company, a nation, or the world. The main driving factors are investment, innovation, skills, new businesses, and competition. But from 1995 to date, capital investment has generally been flat or declining, the quality and quantity of actual labor skills remained the same, and there have been at least two significant economic setbacks. Despite this, productivity has increased. Most mainstream economists agree that technology is the main reason, along with the know-how for converting it into business applications and processes.[50] After an era of anemic productivity growth from the early 1970's to 1995, contrary to the economists' expectations, productivity began to significantly improve in the mid-1990's and has continued to do so today. Between 1971 and 1995, productivity (defined as output per hour worked) grew at only 1% per year.[51] Official forecasts at that time were pessimistic.[52] But then, according to the US Department of Labor statistics, productivity growth soared. Between 1995 and 2004, it was

50 "Productivity," Wikipedia.
51 Bureau of Labor Statistics, 1997.
52 Dale W. Jorgenson, Mun S. Ho and Kevin J. Stiroh, "A Retrospective Look at the US Productivity Growth Resurgence," Journal of Economic Perspectives, Winter 2008, Vol. 22, No. 1, p. 3-24.

more than twice the average of the previous two decades.[53] Even in the aftermath of the 2007-2008 recession, productivity accelerated to almost 4% in 2010.[54] A 2011 McKinsey study showed that use of the Internet accounted for 21% of GDP growth over the previous five years in developed countries and created 2.6 jobs for every job it eliminated. The Internet boosted productivity of small and medium businesses by 10%, and the more a nation used the Internet, the wealthier it became.[55] As this book goes to press, US corporate profits are reaching and surpassing all-time records, the US stock market has exceeded its previous highs, and corporate investment is at a historic peak.[56] To put recent productivity statistics in historical perspective, during the first wave of the Industrial Revolution, 1800's productivity grew at about 1% a year. The average recent growth today is 2.5% a year.[57]

The Bureau of Labor Statistics and prominent economists determined that the main cause of this increased productivity is information technology; that is, the technological progress and its incorporation into the business world. Empirical studies by leading economists conclude that information technology is at the heart of the US productivity resurgence.[58]

Several prominent economists recently responded to the question of why did these significant productivity gains only began in the mid-1990's even though the first commercial computer was introduced

---

53 Dale W. Jorgenson, Mun S. Ho, and Kevin J. Stiroh, "Will the US Productivity Resurgence Continue?" Federal Reserve Bank of New York, (Dec. 2004), Vol. 10, No. 13.

54 Brynjolfsson and McAfee, 30.

55 James Manyika and Charles Roxburgh, "The Great Transformer: The Impact of the Internet on Economic Growth and Prosperity," McKinsey Global Institute, 11 October 2011, www.iei./iu.se

56 Brynjolfsson and McAfee, 3.

57 Ibid., 30.

58 Jorgenson, Ho, and Stiroh, 2008.

in the 1950's. The answer is the fundamental shift in the production cycle of semiconductors with accelerated manufacture of improved chips, which in turn resulted in enormous capital investment. Consequently, productivity and improved company processes using technology increased. Stated another way, companies began making large investments in the new technologies, which made business practices and procedures using those technologies much more efficient.[59] In short, there is now a consensus among economists that, despite the recent economic downturns, the advances in information technology and the incorporation of those technologies into business are the primary reasons for US productivity growth, record corporate profits, and stock market performance.

Looking to the near future, this is simply the tip of the iceberg. The compounding effect of Moore's Law and the other IT laws discussed in Chapter 1 will provide technology that will provide for even greater productivity. But to realize these gains, traditional work methods must change in a profound way. Mankind has previously experienced economic revolutions that have fundamentally changed the way people work and live. The Agricultural and economic revolutions were caused by the economic efficiencies of new advances. They occurred not because leaders of commerce and government decided it was a good idea, but because the productivity from the advances was far superior to the old way. And when change came, it occurred quickly. Consider that upright humans appeared about four million years ago, but that it was only about 12,000 years ago (98 BC) that the Agricultural Revolution began. In other words, for most of the millions of years of human history, man existed as a hunter-gatherer. Work consisted of foraging and hunting for food on a daily basis. That was the work world. The Agricultural Revolution

---

59   Jorgenson, Ho, and Stiroh, 2004 and 2008.

began when people figured out how to domesticate wheat, barley, beans (98 BC), and animals (7,000 BC), made bread using yeast (4,000 BC), and used irrigation (3,500 BC) and wind power (900 AD).[60] With these advances, people were able to live and work in the same location, raising plants and animals in a fundamental change from the nomadic work life. With the British Agricultural Revolution, new technology and agricultural processes converged. In 1700, a seed drill was invented for the systematic planting of crops, and, thirty years later, the first iron plow was commercially sold in Europe. This technology provided a food surplus for the first time in history, permitting people to work in supportive service-related jobs as builders, craftsmen, and shopkeepers. It created wealth, culture, and discretionary time for education, design, music, and literature, and the surplus wealth permitted people to purchase products beyond what they needed to feed themselves. So after four million years of a work world constituted of the nomadic quest for food, it was only twelve thousand years ago that people began living and working in one place, and a mere 300 years ago when life and work completely changed for almost everyone as a result of enormous gains in worldwide wealth from harnessing bioenergy and domesticating plants and animals. It was an entirely new work world.

If the Agricultural Revolution can be considered a very recent event in the context of human history, then the fundamental change in the nature of work resulting from the Industrial Revolution occurred yesterday. The effect of the Industrial Revolution on the average worker occurred around 1830, less than 200 years ago. That is when the technological and economic consequences from the adaptation of railways, steam ships, machines, chemical manufacturing, iron production processes, and machine tools began to touch everyone.

60   "Time Table of Agricultural and Food Technology," Wikipedia.

By the middle of the 1800's, commercial oil production began, and at the end of the century, the diesel engine was patented, leading to cars and airplanes by the first decade of the 20th century. In less than 100 years, almost every aspect of daily work life for most people in the Western world was completely new. With the movement of people to cities and towns where there they performed jobs in factories and offices that for the most part did not exist before, average income and population grew at an unprecedented rate. For the first time in history, "the living standards of the masses of ordinary people have begun to undergo sustained growth ... nothing remotely like this economic behavior has happened before." [61] Lifestyles were completely transformed, with people residing in towns and cities, united for family, friendship, trade, and politics.[62] While in 1900 farming was still a significant portion of work (41%), by 2000 it was only 2% of work. Looking at the mankind's four million year timespan, the jobs and the lives of humans changed in a relative nanosecond from hunting and gathering to laboring in a field behind the plow and raising domesticated animals to working in a factory or behind a desk or in a retail facility.[63]

Both of these economic revolutions were signaled by significant developments towards the end of the previous eras. Near the close of the Agricultural Era in the 1780's, the textile industry and the earliest forms of mass production began in England, providing a window into the future to the Industrial Revolution.[64] While those early indications of revolutionary change did not affect the majority

---

61 Saylor, 228.
62 Saylor, 17, 125, 228; "Industrial Revolution," Wikipedia; George P. Landow, "The Industrial Revolution: A Timetable"; "The Victorian Web," www.victorianweb.org/technology/ir/ichron.html; "The Web Chronology Project, The Industrial Revolution," www.thenagain.inso/webchron/westeurope/indrew.html.
63 Saylor, 229; Brynjolfsson and McAfee, 49-50.
64 "Agricultural Revolution," www.timetoast.com/timelines/agricultural-revolution-.2.

of people who continued to work in farming, it foretold what would happen within 100 years as the work world moved from farms to the cities, completely transforming jobs and lifestyles.

While some scholars believe we have already moved to a new era—the digital revolution or the information age—most people still live and work almost identically to the ways of the Industrial Revolution. The vast majority of people live in cities or towns, arising every morning to travel to a workplace where they perform jobs for a determined number of hours, usually under the supervision of a boss. Digital technologies are simply tools that assist workers in doing the same type of work they would have been doing 30, 40, or 50 years ago. Like the end of the Agricultural Revolution, when new technologies and work processes emerged (such as textile mills and manufacturing) that provided a window into the future, we can now see the future work world if we open our eyes. Just as most people living during the Agricultural Era did not perceive that the nature of work would completely change, and just as the hunters and gatherers did not envision that people would live in a stationary home and work on the same plot of land every day, so too, most of us living in this time do not realize that the way we work and live is about to undergo a profound change.

The corporate leaders and consultants I've spoken with believe the work world will not change. They view the nature of work as something that has been around forever and cannot accept the notion of a revolutionary new work world. But in fact the way we work and live has existed for less than 200 years—a mere moment in the history of man. The powerful technological foundation that will be here in the next few years will change jobs, just as Industrial Age inventions changed work at the end of the Agricultural Era. The transformation that occurred in the Industrial Revolution did not happen because the ruling class decided that it would be beneficial to change work and life. There was no decision to radically alter life and work as it had been for thousands of years. Rather, it happened because of the economic efficiency of using new technologies, such as steam engines, electricity, railroads, and new manufacturing processes (which developed from the new machinery), and which were so overwhelmingly superior that it forced a change. It was during the English Industrial Revolution in the 18th century that economists first measured productivity growth, probably because for the first time in history, growth was palpable and significant (about 0.5% annually).[65]

Today there is the same belief that nothing changes and everything remains the same. In the corporate setting, leaders cling to the rule that employees need to be physically present in a central workplace for training, supervision, and collaboration. In the manufacturing sector, companies still seek cheaper labor by outsourcing to factories in third world countries that function in the same way as they did one hundred years ago. In retail, the leaders continue to support physical stores as the centerpiece of their business. But change is happening right now under the radar screen as employees and companies are beginning to move into a virtual work world. That it is happening now in a limited way, even with flawed and unreliable technological infrastructure, provides a glimpse of what will happen when we have a truly robust technological foundation.

Holly owns a company that oversees large commercial and residential construction projects to make sure the work is proceeding as planned and within the budget. It is a highly complex process in which her company reviews all of the information relating to the project (environmental surveys, zonings, lease negotiations, contracts, and architectural drawings) to determine whether the actual cost of the construction is in line with the projected cost. The companies, banks, and other investors that finance these projects hire Holly's

65   "Productivity Improving Technologies (Historical)," Wikipedia.

firm to make sure that their investment stays within the budget. Most firms like Holly's have regional offices around the country with full-time employees who are sent to the work sites by car or plane, as well as central offices where staff perform analysis of the complex construction documents and data. Her competitors have substantial overhead in bricks and mortar and full-time employees. But Holly's company started about nine years ago with the goal of having as little overhead as possible. They wanted to perform their work in a highly economical way, recognizing that their service did not add value for clients but was necessary for protecting their interests. What Holly's firm created is a business that is almost entirely virtual. The central office located in Chicago is a 600 sq ft space with a monthly rent of $500. Other than Holly and her one partner, there are only three permanent employees—an office manager, an architect who analyzes the complex materials and prepares reports, and another architect who visits construction sites around the country and writes reports. Only the office manager is physically present in the office. Holly works from her home in Toronto or wherever she is and communicates via her computer or her smartphone. The construction site reviews are done by a network of independent contractor architects based all over the country. Many of the architects are women who left traditional firms because they wanted to set their own hours for family reasons. The firm also uses "retired" architects who came from established firms. Holly's company contracts with these architects for projects located in close proximity to where they live.

The firm maintains a very rigorous training program. Most of the training is done by telephone. To teach the new architects how to do the document reviews, they fly to the Chicago office for an extensive three day, onsite training program. When the firm started, documents were all hard copy. Now, 90% of the documents are e-documents in the firm's own electronic document format. Holly feels that her workforce, comprised primarily of women and retired architects, was a neglected group of highly talented people. These are professionals who prize flexibility in their hours and freedom as to where they work. Holly has concluded that they are highly motivated to do a superb job. Her own physical location in Toronto has no connection to the business, which transpires at work sites all around the United States. Holly did not tell her clients when she moved to Toronto because she considered it irrelevant. Given the nature of the business, she has never met any of the borrowers and rarely meets the bankers in person. But through email and phone she maintains strong, and in some cases personal, relationships with them. With her smartphone, she is available to her clients and team 24/7, and she will respond to or initiate contact whether she is at the playground or sitting in her home office. But she is able to "turn it off" when she wants, and so she can maintain a great quality of life. Her company is thriving not because it is virtual but because it is highly efficient and provides great service with top notch talent. Because of the low overhead, the firm can provide lower prices and better service to clients.

Holly's virtual company is not unique. WordPress, one of the top ten software companies in the world, operated without an office until very recently, even though it employed almost 400 people around the world. The founder is based in San Francisco, the creative director lives in a small town in Alabama, and the other employees are scattered in diverse geographies. Communications are primarily through an internal blog and recently through an internal system similar to Twitter where the communications are open to employees. It is a social network type of communication system.

Signal 36, another leading software company, has employees spread out across eight cities on two continents, and even though the "headquarters" are in Chicago, at least half of the employees live elsewhere, including abroad. One of the two key partners is based in Europe, and the other in the US. The company, which provides business software, has no traditional business work structure; that is, no 40 hour work week, meeting schedules, or traditional corporate office culture. The company founder believes that business meetings are an "interruption" of work where people in a room are wasting time. Its meetings are, for the most part, virtual, which permits the participants, if they are not engaged in the discussion, to do other things during the meeting. Jeff Bezos, the founder of Amazon, is the company's only investor.

This shift to the virtual world is not just limited to small companies, however. IBM, one of the most "buttoned up" companies of them all, with its tradition of blue pinstripe employee "uniforms" and large office buildings around the globe, went through much more than a simple transition from a hardware company to a consulting company in the mid-1990's. Faced with the necessity to either reinvent itself or go out of business, almost overnight IBM dropped the blue suits, closed its offices, and enabled thousands of its employees to work from home. This was done at a time when technological tools for virtual working were poor compared to now, just as the current technology will look primitive compared to what it will be in a few years. IBM employees were forced to work in an entirely different way, without corporate offices and by using telecommunication technology to connect with colleagues and supervisors. Bosses were required to assess their subordinates based on an objective assessment of the quality of their work rather than subjectively looking at what they appeared to be doing in the office. All the other subjective measures of job performance became far less important as well. Employees could no longer succeed through superficial, face time activities in the office. With employees working remotely, the company was forced to set real metrics for job performance and eliminate those jobs that did not really add value. To survive and succeed, employees needed to be highly organized and disciplined. Those employees who required "high maintenance" were in trouble. Soon, IBM began to see that the new breed of younger employees who learned in college how to work collaboratively with technology and each other were more effective than many older employees who were struggling to adapt to being untethered from a physical office.

The big story with IBM is that economics acted as the catalyst to transform a traditional business into a substantially virtual business. Today, over 40% of its almost 400,000 global employees do not have a traditional office. Since 1995, IBM has reduced its office space by over 40%, eliminating 78 million of its 185 million square feet. This is not a company where people work at home part time and come into the office to use the infrastructure and report to the boss; rather, the office space is gone, and IBM employees are working virtually. Most significantly, this was not simply a change where the company temporarily cut back on overhead to save itself; instead it transformed itself into a new, far more efficient and profitable entity which is now a dominant, if not the top, company in its field. And it has done this with a workforce that is spread all over the world in an infinite number of locations, connected virtually to one another and working without punching a time clock or operating under the traditional office structure. This transformation was driven by a "burning platform" as IBM faced extinction, which forced its leaders to innovate. What has happened at IBM provides a window into the future as to what will soon happen to the whole work world in a profound way.[66]

66   Janet Caldow, "Working Outside the Box: A Study in the Growing Momentum in Telework," 21 January 2009, www.ibm.com/industries/government/ieg/...working-outside-the-box.pdf; Cathy N. Davidson, "How IBM is Changing Its HR Game," *Harvard Business Review*, (HBR Blog Network), 18 August 2011, http://blogs.hbr.org/cs/2011/08/how-ibm-is-changing-hr-game.html.

But even these leaders, who are already managing companies that are moving to a virtual work environment, do not always recognize what is happening. Donald, an extremely successful healthcare entrepreneur, started an IT healthcare consulting firm in the late 60's, assisting hospitals and other healthcare entities to upgrade their healthcare information systems. He did this very successfully using the traditional consulting model: sending consultants to the physical hospital site, where they would work for weeks or months assessing, advising, and implementing new information technology. He sold his business about ten years ago and began looking for a new business that would not violate his non-compete agreement. After looking at countries around the world, he decided that China could be an excellent customer for the kind of consulting service he could provide. China was in the process of putting in a state-of-the-art infrastructure (airports, railroads, and factories) for its new economy, but its healthcare system was antiquated. He correctly surmised that China would need to upgrade and modernize its healthcare system, which would require consulting assistance for its IT systems. He established a consulting business in China much like his old model, and he hired a staff of five permanent consultants, all of whom were Chinese nationals. Today, the new firm has 25 clients and is growing. Donald still lives in the US, relying on one of his Chinese employees, a 30 year old man, to serve as the "leader" who manages the consulting projects. The young man oversees independent contractor consultants as well as the full-time staff. During my interview with Donald, he shook his head in disbelief when discussing the "unbelievable productivity" of his young number two man and the high quality of his work. Donald believes in the traditional onsite consulting model, but his young leader is managing the consulting projects, at least in part, virtually; that is, he and the staff are not always physically present at the sites. Donald thought that he would simply replicate his consulting firm in China, but his young subordinate created a new model that is far more efficient. Donald believes in servicing his clients the old-fashioned way—boots on the ground—but his young subordinate is serving more clients in less time by working virtually and handling multiple assignments through virtual communication tools.

Donald, like many of our corporate leaders today, does not really grasp what is going on in his own company. He did not institute the virtual component of his consulting firm; rather, it happened organically because the technology was there and the young man running the day-to-day operations wanted to do the work in the most economically efficient way. This is a pattern that we will see over and over and over again in the near future.

Alex is a 34-year-old higher education administrator who graduated from an elite Eastern college in 1999. After college, she moved out to the West Coast to get a job and be close to her sister. She was hired by a public university and eventually became the program assistant for educational programs in the graduate school. It was a complex job, involving scheduling courses, coordinating new and existing programs, dealing with faculty course issues, and assisting medical students. Working in an office across from the new San Francisco baseball stadium, she had one direct supervisor, two bosses over that supervisor, and another employee at her level who sat near her. When the job started, much of it involved telephone calls and face-to-face meetings with her boss, faculty, and students who would come into the office. Thursdays and Fridays were particularly intense because the students would visit the office to discuss their academic programs. But between 2007 and 2011, Alex spent more and more time in her cubicle and in front of her computer screen, substituting face-to-face meetings with email, and spending less and less time on the phone or meeting with students. In the summer of 2011, for personal reasons, she decided she wanted to move back to her hometown in the Midwest. Her boss was upset when she gave her notice, telling Alex that she was so skilled that it would be extremely difficult to find a replacement. Her boss asked her to try working remotely from her new location until either she found a new job or they hired a replacement. Alex agreed. She moved back to her parents' home, put her computer in her old bedroom, and continued working for the university.

Within days, she was working so much that she did not have time to look for another job. Her workday started as soon as she woke up, made coffee, and turned on her computer. She decided to move her computer from the bedroom to the dining room because she wanted to separate her personal space from her work space. Every Thursday, Alex and her boss would have a meeting via Skype to maintain the routine of weekly face-to-face meetings they had had at the university. Alex felt that there was no real difference in their communications on Skype compared to face-to face meetings except that the Skype connection was sometimes lost and they had to continue the conversation by phone. As for working with faculty and students and performing all the other complex tasks that she performed at the university, she could do them just as well from home barring the occasional loss of her Internet connection. Eventually, she replaced the router in her home, which improved the connection. Alex realized that she was actually more efficient at home than she had been in the office because there were no distractions, no commute, and she was fresh and focused when she started working. Most of the people she worked with did not even know she was not in the office. She did not miss lunches or going out to work with her colleagues because she really had not done much of that when she was in the office. Her main emotional reaction to the new virtual work was surprise at how well it worked and how easy it was. "It was really seamless," she told me. Her situation was not completely unique at the university, as there was a medical professor specializing in AIDS research who spent part of his time researching in Africa, part-time at the university hospital, and the rest in a physical office. Alex noticed that the professor never told anyone where he was. She realized that this was deliberate, and, as far as she could tell, his physical proximity or remoteness had no impact on his effectiveness as a faculty member.

After about six months, her employer did find her replacement, but to her surprise, asked her to continue to work because they needed her, and she could do the job without taking up office space. She plans to move on to another job in her hometown, but she is having difficulty extracting herself from her current position because it's a good job and her employer appreciates her work. While no one has performed a quantitative assessment of her productivity since moving 1,500 miles away from her workplace, Alex believes that she is more productive working away from a central office.

All over the world there are people working this way. Many companies do not make this known for reasons of their own, probably because they do not want to set a precedent or think it is inappropriate. I know of a number of lawyers who have moved from their firm's offices when their spouses were transferred. They have continued to work, prosper, and receive promotions, from associate to partner. Their supervisors and the department heads have told me that these lawyers' efficiency and productivity remained at the same high level when they moved away and began working remotely.

Why do people come to a central workplace? During the Agricultural Era, the workplace was the land where the crops and domesticated animals were located. In the Industrial Age, it was where the machines, documents, files, typewriters, computers, bosses, and fellow employees were located. But what will happen when the physical components of the office completely disappear? As Alex's experience illustrates, we are quickly moving towards a work world without paper, filing cabinets, or any of the other physical things that people now think they need to perform their jobs. Colleagues and bosses will be located around the world. The co-workers you need to work with will not be present in your office. With 3D manufacturing, computer assisted design, and robots to perform traditional manufacturing, with sensors "watching" every inch of the factory, there will be little or no reason to be physically present to produce industrial products. I am not suggesting that everyone will be working in their bedrooms or dining rooms like Alex, although some will. There are good reasons why people will continue to go to a separate workplace. A home many not be appropriate because of small size, the presence of family members, or simply because the individual functions better in a space designated for work. Colleagues or collaborators will be physically in the same place, at least on some occasions, for the purpose of performing projects. But the primary reasons why people need to go to a central workplace will end, because none of the things they need to work will be there. The enormous cost of commuting, measured by time, expense, pollution from vehicles, and maintaining brick and mortar buildings will no longer make economic sense. Workplaces will still exist, but in a very different way: close to where people live, with hours of operations determined by the employee, not the employer.

Let's look a little closer at the main reasons why people come to a central office: paper (documents, files, records, and computers) and people. However, we will soon transition into a world where all work-related information will be instantly available, anyplace and anytime, without using today's cumbersome hardware (computers, tablets, and phones). The elimination of paper will be a major factor in this transition. Even now, it is primarily the people over 40 who feel they must have documents in their hand in order to assimilate information—to mark, feel, and touch it. Younger people do almost all of their work on a screen and have little reason to use paper. The adverse economic consequences of paper use are staggering. Papermaking is the third largest user of fossil fuels after the chemical and steel industries.[67] An office worker uses an average of 10,000 pieces of copy paper every year, with a US national total of four million tons annually.[68] The Environmental Protection Agency considers paper mills among the worst polluters of any industry.[69] And the cost of paper has a palpable, detrimental effect on the bottom line of many businesses. For example, *The New York Times* spent about $40 million in paper costs in 2010, a number that could make a difference between profit and loss.[70] The expense of paper, measured in terms of the direct cost to the business and the economic cost to the nation as the fourth largest emitter of greenhouse gases in the US, will be a principal cause for its elimination.[71]

Computers and other tech machinery in the central workplace are also about to become unnecessary, as workers are now rapidly transitioning to tablets and smartphones for work. In the near future, employees will have a virtual screen so they can obtain all of the information they need for work anytime and anywhere without any hardware.

The people we work with (superiors, co-workers, and others) will be increasingly located in different cities and countries. This is already happening, of course, but will become the norm in the near future.

67   Saylor, 43.
68   Ibid., 73.
69   Ibid., 74-75.
70   Ibid., 68.
71   Ibid., 73-75.

As Bill Joy, founder of Sun Microsystems, famously said, "The best talent does not work for your company." What we will see in the near future is companies hiring the best and the brightest regardless of where they are located or whether the company has a physical office in that location. We will also see more and more non-employees working for businesses on a project basis. The current practice of using independent contractors will expand as both businesses and individuals realize it is in their best interest to collaborate for specific projects using the best global talent available.

The current model for companies will not make economic sense when the office to which they are commuting to does not contain anything of value. If their key colleagues are not there and their work tools (documents and computing tools) are all virtual, what economic sense does it make to spend the time, cause pollution, and pay transportation expenses to go to an office? The corporate practice of the last 150 years requiring individuals to get up every morning, travel to an office where they sit for eight hours and then repeat the journey home, will end because it will soon become economically inefficient and wasteful. It is already beginning to happen below the radar screen.

Alex's story is an example how it will not be the corporate leaders who decide one day that people should be working in a different way; instead, necessity and efficiency will bring about the change. Alex's boss's attempt to keep her on during the search for a replacement resulted in the realization for both Alex and her employer that she was equally, if not more, efficient doing her job without being in the central office. If Alex did not need to commute to do her job, do any of the people in her department need to be there? Does anyone in the university need be present in a brick and mortar structure to do their job? In the near future, the answer to that will be "no."

This book is not about working remotely. It is about jobs fundamentally changing in a way that they are completely different. Cheryl, a successful casting director in Hollywood, has already seen this happen with her job and her experience provides another look into the future. Cheryl grew up in the Midwest with dreams of working in the entertainment industry. In 1988, after graduating from college, she heard about an opening for a receptionist in the casting department at Warner Brothers. It seemed like a long shot, but she decided to try. She made a long-distance call to the main number of Warner Brothers and was put through to one of the casting directors, who was sitting around because there was a writers' strike. He told her that she needed to have an interview in order to be considered for a position. She booked a trip to Los Angeles, and, when she arrived at the studio, she was met by the casting director, who said the receptionist job was gone. But much to her surprise, he hired her as an assistant vice president for television casting. She started at $550 per week, and within three years, she was a vice president of casting, making twice that amount. Much of the job involved looking for talent, so she attended theater, comedy clubs, and other live venues where she could see performers. She worked at Warner for five years, then moved to ABC as the head of casting for a mini-series, and then became an independent casting director.

A casting director is an extremely complex job involving artistic skills like directing actors during auditions, as well as understanding each part of the script as it pertains to the roles to be cast, possessing the knowledge and contacts to locate the most qualified actors, and logistically coordinating the scheduling and auditions. It is extremely labor intensive, and it often takes months to complete a project. For example, in 1999 she was in charge of casting for a TV mini-series about a famous rock group. Her task was to recommend performers for about 90 roles. Three full-time people worked for her: an assistant, an associate, and an intern, and the work took two months to complete. As the first step, each role in the script was separated, and a summary was prepared. Rolodexes were then consulted to locate agents, and the summaries were mailed to numerous agents who were expected to submit proposed actors. The agents responded by messenger or mail with the proposed actors' resumes, pictures, and reels (a videotape or film of the actors' previous performances). Cheryl and her staff spread all this information out on tables, chairs, and even the floor. Telephone calls went back and forth between the agents, Cheryl, and her staff. The work was slow, taking several weeks just to gather and sort the files and reels for the hundreds of actors submitted for the roles. Cheryl and her crew debated and finally decided who they wanted to invite in for auditions. Hundreds of telephone calls, calendar entries, and changes occurred. In some cases, the actors would come in and audition for Cheryl and her staff, who would then select the appropriate people to go for a personal audition with the producers and directors. In other cases, she would recommend the actors directly to the producers and directors, in which case the directors, producers, Cheryl, and her staff would gather for an audition where they would sit at a table to watch an actor read for a part. In the end, the studio would make a decision and select an actor for each role. In all, it was eight weeks of intensive, expensive work to cast the mini-series.

Today, Cheryl's job does not resemble what it was in 1999. The end result is the same, but what she does is effectively a new job. Now, Cheryl's work is almost entirely virtual. There are no employees, no staff, no paper, no Rolodexes, no video, and no film. There is very little communication face-to-face or over the phone. And the whole process, which took two months in 1999, now is done in a week or less. Today the script is emailed to Cheryl, who emails it to a website service to do the breakout of the parts. That is done within a few hours, and it is emailed back to her. The web service provides a software program for the entire casting process. The agents are listed online, so Cheryl can instantaneously send the role breakouts to the appropriate agents. Upon receipt, the agents review the material and then use their own software to review their list of actor clients. Usually within hours, they send her, through the software system, all the information she needs regarding the proposed actors: resume, pictures, and reels of their performances. This portion of the process, which previously took days or weeks, now can be done in a morning. Cheryl alone reviews the submissions on her computer screen and selects the actors she wishes to audition. Rather than schedule the actors by phone using a paper calendar, now she does it through a software program called "schedule a session" where she simply puts a date and a time for each actor (one every 15 minutes) with notes as to the location of the session, parking, and all pertinent information about their prospective role. The agent or actor responds through software to confirm, reschedule, or decline the audition. This all can be accomplished in several hours. The actors come to Cheryl's office for the audition, where she has a special camera to record the audition as she directs them. The entire audition is completed within 15 minutes, and the video is automatically uploaded, creating a link that the producers and directors can use to review the audition. They will also receive pictures, resumes, and a demo reel from the actor, through the same link. With auditions occurring every 15 minutes, Cheryl can complete the entire job, even for a multi-part film, in a few days.

The directors and producers who make the selections never see most of the actors in person. They choose the actors based solely on their video auditions. In some cases, Cheryl does not audition the actors live. If they are unavailable to come in, they record their own video auditions and provide the link to Cheryl, who in turn sends it on to the director and producers. She acknowledges that the time may come soon when she will never see any of the actors in person; she believes everything will be done virtually. She contemplates whether this new approach is better or worse than it was 20 years ago. On the one hand, she regrets that some producers or directors will spend only a few seconds looking at a video. In the old days, with a live audition with the actor in the room, the producer and director were forced to watch the entire presentation. On the other hand, because they have videos, they can watch them again, rather than trying to remember what impressed them about someone who auditioned hours or days before. When considering whether it would be even more productive to have all the actors prepare their own video auditions, she says she wants the actors to continue to come to her because she feels that a great casting director will direct the actor to a much better audition than if the actor recorded themselves. But she recognizes that a casting director who insists on doing it the old way would be out of business as no one would pay for that kind of labor-intensive activity anymore.[72] She acknowledges that she never would have made a decision to move into this new high-tech method of casting herself; rather, circumstances forced her into it. She was fortunate that her assistants taught her the new technology so that she could ultimately do all this herself. If she had not transformed herself into a completely different type of casting director, she believes that she would be out of business today.

Bob Reynolds is one of the top saxophone players in the world today, but most people have never heard of him. His story concerns another major component of the coming virtual work world. When Bob began playing jazz professionally in the early 2000's, he was told by

72 The job duties of talent scouting, such as attending clubs and theaters, is now almost exclusively done by searching YouTube for new performers.

his college professors and members of the jazz music establishment that he would be a star. But when he graduated from college, the jazz music business, where it had always been difficult to make a living, suffered a series of blows as the big record companies, under pressure from music pirating, began to severely cut back on their least profitable genres, dropping their jazz artists, even star musicians like Wynton Marsalis. While there had been a revival in interest in jazz in the 1980's and 90's, by the beginning of the 21st century, jazz audiences dwindled, along with the number of performance venues. Bob did not get a record contract and had limited opportunities to perform. Despite the inhospitable environment, Bob's talent was so big that he developed a following. In 2007, a former classmate from Berklee College of Music, pop star John Mayer, asked Bob to join his touring band. But even though Bob was now playing places like Giant Stadium and Madison Square Garden with Mayer and selling out small jazz clubs, he needed to generate more income.

In 2008 Bob did not see things improving, as the recession further dampened his economic possibilities. When on tour that summer with John Mayer, something happened that would change his life. He was backstage having a Skype chat with a cousin and the cousin's two year old son. Bob took out a saxophone and played, and the little boy became extremely excited. Bob had an epiphany: if he could generate such a reaction with a jazzy video over a cellphone, maybe he could do online lessons to supplement his income.

At first, Bob gave lessons in real time on Skype. Within a short period, he had four or five students. But it was not a sustainable business model because it was too random, with no set dates. He decided to consolidate all of the lessons within one teaching day, but that was frustrating for him because he was essentially repeating the same lesson over and over again. He asked himself how he could reach all of the students at the same time without repeating himself through individual lessons. One of his students from Jamaica was a golf pro. He told Bob that he provided very expensive day golf lessons for tourists, but they accepted the expense because they could take home a video of the lesson. Inspired, Bob began experimenting with a different way to get his teaching across online.

In December 2010, Bob played to a packed house at the Hotel Café in Los Angeles. During each break, he checked his cellphone to see what kind of response he was getting on the new teaching website that he had launched that day. The website provided unlimited video lessons for a membership fee. People would be able to access 15 minute instructional videos on an as-needed basis. At the end of the Hotel Café gig, there was $1,500 in his PayPal account from new charter members. Since that time, he has had a 200-400% increase in membership every month. There are now over 160 instructional videos on the website, and he has students from all over the world.

As Bob put more and more videos online, the question then became how to guide the students through the videos and make the instruction something more than simply watching the videos. He noted that many, if not most, of his aspiring sax students were isolated. He considered how to give them engagement in a "community." When he started the online school, he would respond to each individual email from his students, but then he started posting the email questions for everyone to see so the other students could comment or respond as well. This soon evolved into a "chat room" and a social network. For example, Bob would post the question "are you having problems with bebop scales? What are the problems?" This would generate an array of responses, comments, and questions as his students interacted with Bob and with each other. Bob saw that the chat room could be more than people simply communicating in an unstructured way, so he guided the online

Why Technology Will Completely Change the Way We Work

discussions to provide structure based on his teaching methodology and to create a sense of community. He recognized that he had a large group of students generally at the same level with much in common. He viewed the students as a "tribe" and himself as the "tribe leader." He focused the discussions between the participants not only on improving saxophone skills, but also creating a personal connection between all of them.

The big story with Bob Reynolds is not that he created a new business for himself or that he increased his fan base through his online teaching; rather it is that he incorporated social networking like Facebook and Twitter into his school, making technology central to its success.[73]

Before social networking exploded on the Internet, communication was either from one person speaking with another or one person addressing a group or audience. One-on-one communication was accomplished by face-to-face conversation, telephone calls, or email. A single person could address a group by giving a speech or writing a book or an article in a newspaper or by presenting a news broadcast on television or radio. But true interactive communication, where a number of people simultaneously share ideas, facts, or views, was limited to meetings or a teleconference, both of which were dependent on location, scheduling, and physical availability. All the participants had to be available in the same room or on the same phone call. Social networking is an entirely new way of communication. You can have any number of people anywhere in the world simultaneously involved in a discussion, and that discussion can take place in real time or asynchronously. So if someone states her opinion on Facebook by text or video, others can respond immediately, or they can respond at a later point as they see the

---

73 In August 2013, Bob's new album hit the number one position on the iTunes jazz charts.

preserved text or video. Hundreds, thousands, or millions of people can participate in the same conversation. This type of multiple, time-shifted communication never existed before, and it has already had profound effects in the way people communicate socially and in politics. Facebook connects friends and family. Twitter permits an individual to post an idea by text or video, and her followers may respond to the tweeter and all of her followers. The effects of social media have already been profound on world events. The Arab Spring, first reflected by the Egyptian Revolution, would likely not have happened if not for a group of activists connecting on social media about a political leader they opposed.

The profound impact of social media on societal communications will soon have a comparable effect on business communications. In organizations, communications are essentially a top-down process. The leader of a company, department, or project sets up a method of communication that is usually a combination of one-on-one talks or meetings with his subordinates, where assignments and information are conveyed from the boss to the subordinates. All of this is done in a bunker type environment where information is shared selectively, based on what the boss determines. The traditional company is a bureaucracy, and bureaucracies were set up to organize routine production or the performance of tasks. This worked very well in the Industrial Age. But bureaucracies are not good at the complex, interactive projects that comprise much of the work in the highly competitive global business world, where colleagues are located in different parts of the country and world, and the processes of production and performing tasks are extremely complicated. Today, businesses need to innovate and respond to a rapidly changing environment in order to survive. The old model of a boss communicating down to subordinates in a linear fashion, where information is possessed at the top and is fed to the subordinates on an as-needed basis, will not work in this new environment. One can look at almost any business today and see that often the subordinates have valuable information and know more than their superiors about what is necessary to perform the task or objective. This is because information now is transparent and available, and it will become even more so in the future. In the old world of business, information was also shared informally, as employees formed their own social network where they communicated information and ideas by walking down the hallway to talk to colleagues, meet for lunch and socialize after work. But now, with employees in different locations, the old-fashioned informal business social network is dying. Consequently, the traditional corporate communication vehicles are becoming archaic and unproductive.

In the near future, social networking will move into the business realm, becoming the primary means by which individuals perform their jobs. Ninety nine percent of employee communications will be through a virtual site where literally everything needed for the job will be instantaneously available. The site will provide an ongoing meeting and communication hub where everyone's work will be available in an ongoing basis.

Social networking in the business world will constitute what I call "the ongoing meeting." Within an organization, there will be numerous networks designed for particular purposes. There may be a network for everyone in the company where general information and news is shared, commented upon, and where questions are posed. Work projects will have their own network where all of the participants are connected. On a particular project network, all data and documents will be instantly available, and each document will show all of the notes, observations, and modifications provided by any of the project members. Project members will communicate by text, video, or any other means they so choose. The network can also be used for periodic "live" meetings where people participate via video. Those meetings will be "recorded" and made accessible in the future to anyone who missed the meeting or wished to review, add, or revise the information. Anything provided to the network will be available on an ongoing basis and located through a sophisticated algorithm-based search tool. The network might give individuals the option to delete communications that they no longer think is relevant or wish to modify.

Let's consider the significance of the ongoing meeting. It will level the playing field, permitting collaboration, sharing of information, and exchange of ideas in a way never available before. When employees at different levels of the organizational hierarchy are participating in an ongoing meeting, the confines and restrictions of the person's job are lifted. Since all the connected individuals can participate with their ideas, facts, and other input, their job descriptions have less significance, and they are not limited by the artificial box of that description. Given the advantages of tapping into a broader, bigger human resource pool—more employees who can add value to the project—companies will welcome more people into the ongoing meeting so that it can benefit from a larger source of input and creativity.[74] The individual worker will be judged by the substance of their contribution rather than their job title, who they report to, what they look like, or whether they are a good dinner companion.[75] All that irrelevant "stuff" that gets in the way of an efficient, creative, and productive work force will diminish in importance as the ongoing meeting business network becomes the norm. Actual contributions will become the only thing that counts. Parenthetically, the skill set

74   Jim Harris, *Blindsided*, (Capstone, 2002).
75   "Nothing to Fear: Apps for Tracking Workers' Productivity," *The Economist*, 14 October 2013.

that has traditionally been considered a strength of female employees (the ability to adopt to changing work environment, teamwork, and strong communication skills that combine empathy, compassion, articulateness, and flexibility) will be essential assets in the virtual business world. Attributes that have traditionally hurt women in work, such as physical presence, high voices, or physical strength (in factory jobs), will become irrelevant in the virtual world. We are already seeing evidence of this as middle-aged men, who have traditionally held the supervisory and managerial jobs, are laid off and then are unable to adapt and change sufficiently to get different work while female salaried employees advance in the new online business world.[76]

The ongoing meeting business network will also change the role of leaders. There will not be a straight-line hierarchy but rather a collaborative environment where the leaders act as guides and facilitators. Certainly the bosses will retain the authority to make the ultimate decisions to hire and fire people, and to promote and demote. But the transparency of the ongoing meeting network will provide objectivity in judging individual contributions that did not exist before. Since each individual work product will be available to everyone, employees can be judged on their merit. More importantly, each person's work can be viewed and improved by everyone in the network. All of the normal constraints of time and distance will be eradicated because the opportunity to share information and provide ideas among the network never ends as long as the project continues. The ongoing meeting business network will change the nature of leadership, being a worker, and work itself.

The technology currently exists to have such business networks, and some companies are doing it, but the real tipping point will come

76   Hanna Rosin, *The End of Men* (Riverside Books, 2012).

soon with more robust technology to make information available in an effortless, instantaneous manner with seamless text and video communications. Microsoft has quietly been spending billions assembling the components for a robust social/business network foundation, buying Yammer, a software company that permits employees to collaborate on projects, share files, and chat, and by buying Skype, the online video conferencing company.[77] There are now a number of medical and healthcare business social networks. One is Doximity, which enables referring doctors and specialists to communicate and share records on an ongoing basis.[78] IBM now has a "social software" consulting unit.[79] Quirky is a manufacturer that creates products by having its own designers work with inventors from all over the world who submit inventions and then collaborate through the network to create, manufacture, and distribute products such as kitchen tools, bathroom accessories, and storage crates.[80] The giant business software company SAP just spent over $4 billion to buy a business networking marketplace to provide a global network of sellers and corporate buyers on an international scale. SAP takes a percentage of the profits for any transaction for providing a foundation for an international network of buyers and sellers to communicate regarding their products. At present, there are almost three quarters of a million vendors, and it's growing at about a thousand companies per week.[81] That we are seeing these companies putting billions of dollars into these technologies further evidences the fact that we are on the verge of a revolutionary change in business processes and the way we work. [82]

---

77 "Microsoft Buys Business Only Social Network," *New York Times*, 30 November 2012.
78 "Social Media Tools Can Boost Productivity," *USA Today*, 12 August 2012.
79 Ibid.
80 "Social Design Site Quirky Launches US Made Product," *USA Today*, 13 June 2012.
81 "SAP's Marketplace Dream," *New York Times*, 2 November 2012.
82 "Social Media Tools Can Boost Productivity," *USA Today*, 12 August 2012.

Just as email rapidly replaced postal mail and telephone, so too will business networking replace one-to-one communications. Business networks will bring about organizational structural changes by flattening hierarchies, providing less rigid reporting relationships, and fostering more informal work cultures. We will see employees work across departments and divisions because those who possess relevant knowledge, judgment, and expertise will no longer be physically limited to a particular area of the company as technology enables them to easily work in different areas on multiple projects. Companies with rigid workplace cultures that limit this type of collaboration will be disadvantaged. Those companies that have a culture that is open to business social networks will succeed.

While Facebook, Twitter, and other social networking sites are illustrative of how businesses will communicate, online gaming provides another window into the future. Online gaming is comprised of an immense social network with thousands of players in a particular game working together to win the game. Of course, collaborating with colleagues is what we do at work, but the difference with online gaming is that the people playing the game are part of a social network. The online gaming world provides insight as to where and when people will work. Some play games at home alone, while others play physically in the same location, permitting them to personally interact with fellow gamers (who may be involved in a different game) while at the same time working virtually and interacting with thousands of others around the world. This is how people will work—alone or in work spaces with others while at the same time virtually with fellow workers around the world.

So the workplace of the near future will involve working in the virtual world and the real world simultaneously. We are, after all, social animals who thrive on being with other people, and that will continue in the future work world. However, virtual interactions will be the primary means of communication in the new work world. It will be like a telephone switchboard where everyone will interact with everyone else simultaneously, sharing information and having access to all that is going on.

There is a business theory that the best and smartest people work for someone else, and that companies are staffed with the employees that they were able to hire.[83] One of the reasons, perhaps the main reason, why companies cannot hire the very best, even when they have enormous economic resources, is that companies cannot be physically located everywhere. For example, accounting firms, even those with numerous offices, are still limited to hiring people residing near their office locations or willing to move to those locations. In the near future we will see the creation of a new multinational accounting firm that recruits the best and the brightest professionals regardless of location. It will become a leading, perhaps the dominant, accounting firm, dispensing with the burdensome and expensive brick and mortar infrastructure by substituting technological infrastructure where accountants work and service their clients virtually with lightning fast access to all of the information and documents they need anytime, anywhere, conducting business via virtual meetings. They will be able to service clients anyplace, anytime, anywhere in a superior fashion and far cheaper and faster than a traditional accounting firm.

In the near future, as business networks become the norm and work is done virtually, it will not matter where people are located or whether they are permanent, part-time, independent contractors, or unpaid interns. The best people are located everywhere, and their abilities may or may not be reflected by their educational level, prior

83 Anderson, 143.

job achievements, or any other standard metric of achievement. The business network, via the ongoing meeting, will help redefine what a workforce is, as it will permit companies seek out the best and the brightest for their workforce regardless of location. There will be less permanency in a workforce because the best participants may be brought in for the project at hand and then move on when the project is completed. These changes will be driven not by a decision by a corporate leader, but by the enormous efficiencies and productivity resulting from seamless communications between the best and brightest workers tapping into all of the information they need for the job while working anytime, anyplace, and anywhere.

CHAPTER 3

Who?

If not corporate leaders, who then will lead the change in the way we work? I have talked about how our business leaders and managers are for the most part blind to what is occurring. Some throw up roadblocks to prevent younger employees from working virtually. There is the boss who tells his employee that she must be in her office, at her desk, from 8:30 to 5:00 every day and that all reports need to be printed and placed on his desk. This boss is puzzled when the employee suggests that the documents and information should be available in an eRoom, easily accessible to everyone on the project. Even if the boss agrees to online access, he does not even know how to access the E-files himself. Then there is the manager who tells his executive secretary not to waste time getting trained on the new office software because she won't need it in her job assisting him. And there is the CEO who tells the head of the corporate IT department that the current software, even though badly outdated, is good enough.

In my interviews for this book, almost every corporate leader and manager disagreed with my premise that the nature of work is changing and there will be a profound change in the work world in the near future.[84] They all argued that because things have always been this way, they would remain the same. Never mind that the work world has not always been this way as the work methods of

84   70% of Fortune 500 CEOs do not use any social networks; CEO.com study: Twitter, LinkedIn Emerge as Top Social Channels for Business Leaders, www.domo.com/news/press-releases/new-CEO-Study-twitter, August 7, 2013.

the Industrial Revolution have only been around for a short period of time in the context of human history. These leaders cannot see what is currently happening right before their eyes. I keep thinking about how the successful consultant entrepreneur who set up a new operation in China could not understand how his thirty-year-old number two man could manage multiple consulting projects so quickly and efficiently. He envisioned that his subordinate was managing it the old-fashioned way by putting consultants on the ground at specific projects, preparing paper reports, and then moving on to the next project. He did not realize that the teams were quickly moving from project to project using virtual technology. While he recognized that their productivity had substantially improved compared to 20 years ago, he did not understand why. And when I asked him about the application of technology in his field, he scoffed at its usefulness.

Rupert Murdoch, of all people, used the phrase "digital natives," referring to people who have grown up in the digital world. These are the individuals born after 1983 who have always used a computer as an integral part of their social, school, and work life. For this cohort, the digital world is part of their DNA, and the younger the individual, the more deeply it is imbedded into their essence.

These digital natives are now coming of age in the work world, and their influence is just beginning to have an effect. They do not vocally champion the virtues of working virtually; they just do it. They are the leaders of a silent revolution. Their bosses are impressed at their efficiency, their ability to find relevant information almost instantaneously, and their skills at preparing a detailed and complex analysis or memoranda in a fraction of the time that their older co-workers do it. But the bosses really don't understand *what* they are doing. Conduct your own informal survey of employees in your office and their use of paper documents. I would bet that you will find the same thing that I did: there is a strong correlation between age and the use of paper. Young employees will only use paper if they have to; that is, if the software systems will not allow them to access, manage, or manipulate content, or if their bosses require that they use paper. The older the employee is, the more likely he is to have paper on his desk. This may not appear to be a big deal, but working in a virtual work world involves giving up the traditional business tools such as paper, pens, files, and filing cabinets. Increasingly, young people do not want to use these things.

Another basic work procedure of the Industrial Age work world is talking to co-workers face-to-face or over the telephone. But young people have grown up in a social world where their friendships and romantic relationships are as much virtual (through text, Facebook, Twitter, YouTube, and Instagram) as they are face-to-face. For them, conducting business by oral communications will be considered unnecessary and wasting waste of time. Digital natives, people born after 1983, will be the drivers of the change in the way everyone works. This generation has grown up with virtual technology, and it is their world.

In today's workplace, there is a vast generation gap between the digital natives and their older colleagues and bosses. These two groups approach work in entirely different ways: the younger group naturally works virtually, while the older group is bound to traditional work methods. This is a silent but profound generation gap. The younger people do not talk about the fact that they work in a different way, nor do they challenge their older colleagues or tell them how inefficiently they are performing by doing things the old way.

Baby-boomers whom I interviewed, including brilliant leaders of corporations, told me that new technologies were just tools to help people perform their jobs. However, when I expressed my views about the coming of a virtual work world to the younger people, they nodded their heads in agreement, as if what I was suggesting was an obvious truism. Many of them are already working virtually to the extent that their companies permitted them to do so or doing so under the radar. They are quietly redefining how jobs are performed.

Sarah graduated from an elite Eastern college during the 2008 recession but was fortunate enough to get a job as an analyst with a wealth management group within a multinational bank. She reported to a group of highly successful wealth managers whose clients had multimillion dollar portfolios. Her bosses quickly recognized her aptitude with computers, particularly her ability to quickly access arcane financial information to assist in making investment decisions. Soon she began performing extremely sophisticated research and analysis of the clients' investment portfolios. Because of her acumen and speed in the virtual world, particularly the ability to instantly access relevant financial data, perform complex analysis, and use her own growing expertise to make judgments and recommendations in collaboration with the technology, she was able to perform far more efficiently and effectively than co-workers who used conventional methods. Within a year or so, she was making the recommendations to her bosses, who accepted her advice so that she was effectively making the investment decisions herself. In other words, she had quietly taken over managing hundreds of millions of dollars of client investment portfolios. Her ability to quickly obtain enormous amounts of information and formulas resulted in a more objective way of making the investment decisions, with less subjectivity and intuition than the traditional investment management approach. From the outside, nothing had changed in the way her group managed the clients' assets, but in fact it was now being done differently. This change did not come about because the bosses decided that it would be better to manage these assets in a different way; rather, it happened because a digital native knew how to find and analyze the entire virtual world of financial information.

Sherry Turkle, a professor at Massachusetts Institute of Technology, studies human technology interaction. Over the past 20 years, she has conducted a number of groundbreaking studies on the effect of technology on people, exploring the topic from an anthropological as well as a psychoanalytical perspective. While her studies focus on social interactions, her conclusions provide great insight into the coming work world. In one of her studies, focusing on young people from the ages of five to their early twenties, Turkle observes that the connection between young people and technology is "nothing less than the future unfolding."[85] Referring to a 2010 Nielsen study that the average teen sends over 3,000 text messages a month (a number that is still steadily increasing), Turkle's research of teens reveals that their social life is more virtual, that is, through use of text and social media communications, than it is real. Teenagers now ask each other out on dates and break up by text.[86] Their text communications reflect intense emotional feelings. Text, Facebook, and other social media now provide a primary means of connecting friends and romantic relationships.[87] Teen etiquette requires texting rather than telephoning. An entire language has been built up around text communications. The time of day that a text is sent by a teenager also carries a subtext. Texts sent during the evening imply greater seriousness than a text sent during the day, which suggests

---

85 Sherry Turkle, *Alone Together: Why We Expect More From Technology and Less From Each Other* (Basic Books, 2011), xiv.

86 Ibid., 197.

87 Ibid., 171-175.

a more informal context. If a teenage girl texts a boy during the evening, it may suggest a romantic interest, while during the day, the message is perceived as a conversation between friends. With virtual communication, the medium is the message. Emotions and communications via text may be provided without any particular content. For example, "whassup?" sends a particular message. There are skilled ways of flirting via text.[88] People use friends to help them in romance just like Cyrano de Bergerac. On online chat rooms, Facebook, and other social networking sites, Turkle's research shows that teenagers can form extremely strong personal relationships with people they've never met.[89] That a Notre Dame football star, apparently the victim of a hoax, could fall in love with a girl who did not exist may seem unfathomable to a middle-aged person, but such intense online relationships are very much part of the social world of teenagers.[90] Young people shift seamlessly from virtual to face-to-face communications so that in many cases they cannot remember whether a particular conversation was in person or virtual.[91] For them, it is all fundamentally the same.

For young people, location is portable and mobile. In the 1960's, when a baby-boomer visited Europe she was separated from her home, family, and friends. Because she was no longer in seamless communication with them, she was transported into an entirely different world. When teenagers today go to Paris, they remain connected with friends and family. As Turkle puts it, we now bring our homes with us when we travel. In some ways, the teen does not even know they're away because they continue to live in the same

88   Ibid., 198-201; Sherry Turkle, "Disruptions: Texting Your Feelings Symbol by Symbol," *New York Times*, 18 August 2013.
89   Turkle, 248-251.
90   "Notre Dame Says Story About TE'O Girlfriend Dying Apparently a Hoax," *Calgary Herald*, 17 January 2013.
91   Turkle, 248-251.

virtual space as they did when they were at home. Going to Paris no longer involves displacement, because the teens' social environment does not really change as she travels.[92]

For young people, the gaming world, where they play complex, ongoing games, provides a virtual environment offering a social life and a collaborative environment as they communicate with other gamers. This world is all-encompassing as gamers spend hours each day living in a parallel universe that is as real to them as the physical world.[93]

Overall, Turkle's research shows that digital natives are different than people over 35 or 40. Today, their social world is completely different, just as their work world will be. We are seeing this already with young people in the workplace. They will be the future game changers of the work world.

Here are some of the ramifications. As younger people now live in a social world where physical location is almost irrelevant to what they do, the central workplace or any particular workplace is becoming more and more unnecessary to them in the performance of their jobs. Just as their social life travels with them wherever they are, their work life will be portable and will exist regardless of time or place. The notion that one needs to have a structured physical work environment with set hours is already belied by successful students today who work virtually with their computers, tablets, or smartphones in cafes, at home, anyplace, and at any time. Students tell me that there is no real need for them to physically attend college lectures if those same lectures are available online. I interviewed one individual at an elite law school who had travelled across the country during the middle of the semester to visit family for three

92   Ibid., 156.
93   Ibid., 157-159.

weeks, missing nothing, he said, because all of the lectures were available virtually.

Turkle talks about the new sense of place. It used to be that if you went to a coffee shop people would be drinking coffee and engaging in the activities related to that experience. Now, in a café, almost everyone is on their computer or smartphone. They are in a different space, engaged in recreation, work, and/or family matters. This is a window into the future of the work world, and young people will lead the change because they already live this way.[94]

This is an argument I so often hear from corporate executives: the social interactions and personal connections from being in the same physical office, meeting at the coffee machine, and going out to lunch cannot be replaced when workers are physically separated. But this is belied by the completely different social world that young people inhabit. I believe that Turkle's studies effectively show that the language and the emotional intensity of communications in the young's virtual social world will inevitably be imported into the new business networking world, where workers will communicate with the same effectiveness, clarity, and emotion that they would if they were together. The way young people live today in a virtual world will be a major catalyst for the paradigm change in the way everyone works.

Skills that young people have developed to text and communicate through social networks will transfer to the work world in a way that may provide more business-like communications than older workers are able to engage in. Turkle's studies show that teenagers talk about how texting offers a feeling of protection, as they have time to think about and prepare what they are going to say. Teens

94   Ibid., _.

understand that they can control how they are portrayed by choosing the right words and carefully editing their text messages. They understand the significance of the subtext of communication. This is, of course, precisely the essence of effective business communication. In today's business world, face-to-face communications, telephone communications, and email communications that are too often spontaneous, emotional, and not well thought out result in wasteful and counterproductive work. We see this every day in the way people deal with one another. Digital natives who have been brought up with virtual communications intuitively understand the pitfalls of poorly thought out communications.[95]

In the same way, Turkle's studies indicate that young people may understand the privacy issues inherent in virtual communication better than middle-aged people. They've grown up with cyber stalking, and many have learned that any communication on social networks can be seen by anyone and can have long term adverse personal ramifications. They realize the dangers of virtual communications and take appropriate precautions. They know that being transparent is a large part of their social life but that they must exercise care.[96] As we move to business networking, there will be transparency among workers in a way that has never existed before. With traditional one-on-one communications, there was an expectation of privacy. But with the ongoing business network meeting, every participant's communications and actions will be seen by everyone else in that network and preserved for later viewing. There will be no place to hide. This is a good thing, because in a business setting where people are working on a project, true productive collaboration requires seeing who is contributing and what she is contributing to the project. Young people have grown

95 Ibid., 200.
96 Ibid., 253.

up with this and understand and accept this openness, but they also have practice and experience in being careful; that is, guarding against spontaneous and poorly thought out communications, recognizing that anything committed to the social network remains there forever and appreciating that the advantages of collaboration outweighs concerns about privacy. With digital natives, there will be self-surveillance at work because as small children, as they learned to type online, soon discovered that typing was forever. They internalized that every misstep was preserved in cyberspace and that the Internet never forgets.[97] Older people, raised in a world where a verbal utterance is impermanent and can be forgotten or at least denied, have had a very difficult time learning that their online communications do not go away.

Based on her research, Turkle concludes that, tethered to the network, people have a new state of self where they are experiencing the physical and virtual world simultaneously and that multi-tasking is the 21st century alchemy.[98] This is the world young people live in, and it will be the world they work in. People will shift from work to play to social interactions to family in a seamless manner. The result will be a much more productive and efficient work world and an enhanced quality of life as the worker is unchained from the constraints of a physical work place and inflexible working hours.

Turkle's studies are not only significant in terms of studying how people relate to each other in a virtual sense through texting and social networking but also how they relate to computational objects themselves. In studies conducted in the 1980's, children began to think of the state of aliveness as whether an object could think on its own; that is, the autonomy of the machine in thinking, acting,

97   Ibid., 259.
98   Ibid., 155.

---

moving and talking. Turkle contrasts this with a 1920's research project where aliveness was viewed as whether something could move; that is, if a cloud moved and a dog moved, they were both alive. In the recent studies, children reacted emotionally when they understood they could stop a little robot from talking by simply taking out the batteries. When they removed the batteries, they believed they would be "killing it." These studies showed that children saw the essence of the computer as the same stuff of which life is made, reflected by a five-year-old girl referring to a tiny digital creature by saying "Well, I love it."[99] In these studies, children spoke of computers as being "kind of alive" and expressed a "kind of love" for robots. They quickly understood that to get the most out of a robot they had to pay attention to it and assess its emotional and physical state. They believed that if they loved the robot, they would be loved in return.[100]

In addition to the emotional connection of children with computers and robots, Turkle's studies showed that teenagers readily placed great confidence in the ability of robots and computers to understand what they needed and to provide better and more comprehensive information than a human would. She illustrates this with an example of a boy who felt confident that the robot would be better able to advise him on the intricacies of his social life because its database would be larger and its artificial intelligence would be more attuned to his exact needs than his dad.[101] Her studies showed that young people trusted that artificial intelligence could accurately monitor their emails, calls, web searches, messages, and supplement their information by its own searches to help them.[102] Overall, her

99   Ibid., 26-28.
100   Ibid., 40.
101   Ibid., 51.
102   Ibid., 51-52.

studies show that young people relate to robots and computers as machines *and* as living creatures. When the computer is in robotic human-like form, it inspires a greater intensity of feeling than using a computer screen. The human body form makes the difference.[103] Young people believe that if they care for their technological tools, the tools, in turn, will care for and help them. They trust that a robot can learn information about them and can be trusted to know about their life.[104]

What is the significance of all this for jobs and work? It is that the younger people are primed to most fully embrace the artificial intelligence that will soon become available, and they will readily collaborate with this technology in their jobs. Powerful chips, sensors, and cloud capacity that will soon provide the foundation for artificial intelligence will give us work assistants who will, in response to a worker's request, provide any information that a person needs to do their job. Imagine the manager of a small paper manufacturer receiving a list of matters that need to be performed in a suggested priority, along with reminders of relevant conversations, preferences of her boss and co-workers of how they want the project delivered, and all other information needed to do the day's work, all from her robotic assistance. The manager sits in her office next to her robotic assistant and converses with it about information she needs to know for a presentation, and the robot provides data to the manager in whatever form she wishes; for example, projecting video on the wall with a checklist of the components of the presentation. The robotic assistant may suggest to the manger that certain aspects of the scope of the presentation were not clearly articulated by her boss and then set up a communication with the boss to clarify. Or the assistant might independently research additional information

103 Ibid., 133-141.
104 Ibid., 141-142.

that manager may need and provide it to her instantaneously. Or this assistant could be virtual: voice and/or text projecting information on any surface regardless of where the manager is physically located.

Digital natives will intuitively trust artificial intelligence assistants, and they are primed to have an emotional connection with them that will make the work pleasant because they will feel that the robot is "almost alive." They will have the knowledge and confidence to "train" the assistant to understand their work to best serve them. The artificial intelligence assistant will be programmed to learn what best serves its "boss," how the "boss" best assimilates information, what format is best to provide information, and what the "boss's" work habits are. In prioritizing work, the assistant will learn whether the "boss" is more effective starting with the more difficult projects first each day, or if it is better to gradually bring her into the day's work flow. The robotic assistant will also learn to identify aspects of the job tasks that are ambiguous, requiring more judgment in determining how they should be done. Young workers—the digital natives—will understand that these robotic assistants are not just technological tools but true collaborators and that effective work requires collaboration between humans and computers.

Recent studies show that collaboration is a major catalyst for productivity. Young people have been the primary users of crowdsourcing, which employs the online world to tap into essentially anyone who can contribute value to a task at hand for a global collaboration. Scientific studies show that a slime-like organism can work its way through a complicated maze more effectively than a human. It is the working together of separate neurons in the slime that achieve a better result than a single human. The human brain is essentially a neuron set connected by electrodes working together.[105] Crowdsourcing operates in an analogous fashion, and it has produced extraordinary results in solving difficult scientific problems by using technology to solicit the collective intelligence, innovation, and wisdom of people all over the world. We are seeing that crowdsourcing, which effectively creates a global collaboration of neurons, produces better and faster results than individuals working alone or in small groups. Young people have grown up in a collaborative world and are ready to work this way. They grew up using gaming to work together to solve complex tasks and attended universities and colleges that taught and tested collaboration in academic projects. The most innovative companies are now recognizing the power of such collaboration. Business networks in the corporate world will bring together diverse global talent and expertise to produce better and faster results.

Earlier in the book I talked about my experiences as an employment lawyer observing how employees were increasingly defining their own jobs and in effect created their own job descriptions. In the near future, the availability of extraordinary new technology will enable workers to significantly mold and shape the way they work, and it is the young people who will be the pathfinders into this new work world.

105 PBS, "Nova Science Now: What are Animals Thinking?," 8 November 2012.

Who?

CHAPTER 4
Jobs of the Near Future

So what will the work world of the near future look like? When I started this chapter, I envisioned that it would contain descriptions of various jobs of the future, but I soon realized that such a litany would make for dull reading. So I decided to present the impending work world in a different way—as the following fictional account narrated by a manager of a furniture manufacturing company describing work and life in the near future:

"I was worried. PI Furniture, a chain of retail furniture stores that I had been talking to for months about buying an exclusive line of my company's office furniture, just told me that they were probably going with another company, one that offered better technological support than my company could provide. I had been just about to close a deal to sell them a sizable order of furniture specifically tailored for their Indonesian retail market. My design team had invested a lot of time creating unique furniture that would fit the smaller physiques of PI's consumers and appeal to the consumer aesthetic preferences of that market. We were also providing technology that would allow the retail consumer to virtually design room furniture layouts in accordance with their own actual room size, windows, and personal preferences. The store customer would use our surround screen technology to place the furniture in a virtual room that replicated the customer's own space and then move the furniture around to see exactly how the pieces would look. The customer could also customize the furniture on the screen by making it smaller or larger to perfectly fit the room. Potential customers visiting a PI retail store could access my company's virtual room technology from a secure cloud and work with a sales/design representative to assist them in planning the office.

I had put an enormous amount of time and effort working with PI Furniture executives on the potential sale. They had been enthusiastic and ready to enter into a long-term contract. I could not understand why they had done a sudden about-face or how another company could have more advanced technology than ours.

My company produces furniture of all types, but it is office furniture that has been driving our growth and prosperity over the last several years. With the demise of the big corporate central and regional office buildings and the new practice of individuals working out of home offices or local rented office space, the demand for custom office furniture had exploded. In many cases, companies are providing stipends for employees to purchase or rent furniture for their home or local office, allowing workers to select the type of furniture that suits them and fits their workspace. My company is now the leader in the worldwide office furniture market. The president of the office furniture division, Bill Baxter, had spearheaded the initiative to produce furniture that would appeal to office workers all over the world. His concept is that people can choose from our vast array of furniture designs, which they can modify through a computer assisted design technology to fit their body type and their room. The customer may choose any fabric or material for the furniture assuming the structural integrity of the product is maintained. So we are able to offer, for example, contemporary Indonesian type designs for PI's customer base and 1950's modernism for other customers' Western European market. We are also offering our own furniture designs, which we developed with our small team of in-house designers who review designs submitted by any independent designer who wished to participate from anywhere around the world. If our designers decide that a submitted design is promising, they work with the outside designers to refine it and ultimately make it available to our retail store customers or directly to individual consumers. Because we only manufacture on demand, when someone orders a piece, the risk of being stuck with a line of furniture that no one wants is not a problem. Consequently we have no real warehousing overhead and have incredible flexibility in our operations. Bill Baxter is the person who has aggressively pushed the company to use the newest technology, crowdsourcing to develop new designs, and other innovations. He is the golden-haired boy of the company.

I started with the company three years ago as a manufacturing manager. The job turned out a lot different than my previous manufacturing jobs. In the past, I worked in a factory overseeing production. But this company does not own factories; it produces the furniture using a global network of manufacturers, vendors, designers, and whatever other resources we need. We use so many different fabrics, metals, woods, and plastics from sources all over the world that I can't begin to even count the thousands of vendors that supply them. The company outsources to factories ranging from high-end production facilities to third world handmade shops to single machine garage shops that "print" chairs. I spend most of my time supervising the factories, suppliers, designers, and other resources to produce the furniture for our retail store and individual customers. Bill Baxter, the president of our division, had the vision to determine that our work could be done using the amazing technology available to us.

For most of my work day, I am involved in an ongoing virtual meeting, in perpetual contact with every individual on whatever furniture project I happen to be working on. If I had to physically visit all of the customers, vendors, production factories, and designers on each project, they would take far longer to complete at a much higher cost. But with our virtual communications process, I'm pretty much able to work seamlessly with whomever I consider the best resources, anywhere in the world, to make the high quality furniture fast and cheap. What I envisioned would be a traditional factory managerial position when I took the job has turned into a worldwide, virtual, logistical supply chain job. [106]

In reality, my job is many jobs requiring skills that I had not developed before. Of course, there is the financial aspect of figuring out the best price, profitability, and all the other accounting components of the project. Sophisticated software allows me to instantaneously run cost comparisons and profitability models when I am assessing a vendor's bid. Our software also monitors each vendor on an ongoing basis as they produce their part of the project so I can always see the costs of production. Coordinating production with the manufacturing staff around the world requires interpersonal skills that I have worked hard to develop. Most of the people I work with are from foreign countries, particularly Latin countries. In many cases, we do not speak the same language. Fortunately, the translation software imbedded into our ongoing meeting network is perfect. It does text and audio translations instantaneously. Sometimes I worry that I may miss language nuances, and for that reason I am taking a Spanish course. I use my engineering degree in my work as I oversee every detail of production, relying on thousands of tiny cameras and sensors imbedded throughout the

106 Peter Marsh, *The New Industrial Revolution* (Yale University Press, 2012), 77, 215-216.

Jobs of the Near Future?

manufacturing and supplier facilities that we use around the world. With the cameras and sensors, I can continually monitor everything going on in the production process and communicate with the people running the factories. In some instances, I directly control robots doing the factory production. Design is one job skill that I did not think that I would be using, but the nature of what we are offering requires me to not only work with designers, but also to use the computer assisted design (CAD) to the modify the designs myself. Just the other day, a customer in Peru wanted slightly wider armrests for one of our standard chairs. I was able to play around with the virtual three-dimensional model of the chair while the customer was with me in the ongoing meeting. Together we were able to run simulations putting virtual people in the chair to see how it worked from a comfort and work practicality perspective. Once we were satisfied, I virtually presented the modified chair to our designers to make sure that I had not compromised the design in any way. It turned out I did a pretty good job.

My job also involves a big dose of customer relations. While I never considered myself a salesperson, once I got into the job it was clear that there is no line between manufacturing a product and satisfying the customer. In order to meet customers' needs, I have to communicate with them every single day. Recently, a prospective account that we were in danger of losing was referred to me based on a recommendation from another customer who thought I was a sales representative. Our division president wants us to be all things to all people, and, most importantly, to satisfy the customer in whatever way they want and do whatever is necessary to work efficiently with our partners, suppliers, and producers. In this company, there are several hundred mangers who have a similar job to mine—overseeing production for our many furniture product lines. In the three years I've been here, I have seen many of them fail, because they either can't or won't be flexible in performing the many functions that are required by our division president. A very good friend of mine was fired because he kept insisting that his job was limited to supervision of the manufacturing process. He thought his job was secure because he was very good at the manufacturing process, but he was wrong. The company decided that there were better people out there who could perform the many necessary functions to serve the customer. I've seen many middle-aged managers fail because they were just too rigid in their approach to the job. I look around and see this company changing very quickly, and I appreciate that in order to keep my job and progress the way I think I should, I've got to keep reinventing myself—learning new things and unlearning obsolete things.

Today I've got a big concern—the apparent loss of a major potential customer, PI Furniture. Sitting in my office, I wave my finger in the air to pull up a virtual surround screen. On that screen, I enter an ongoing virtual meeting of my division. I am encompassed by a screen where I can view text, video, documents, and any information I may need. I can see all communications from my colleagues, bosses, suppliers, or anyone who has access to the ongoing meeting. I can participate in conversations currently going on, or I can scroll back to view or hear past communications. So I have in front of me a record of everything, past and present, regarding the division, and it is all transparent to each participant.

When I enter the ongoing division meeting, I see a video conversation going on in real time between two of my fellow managers, who are discussing the best providers of leathers in Eastern Europe and a running text of a department meeting on whether to put more sales effort into selling office furniture in Brazil. Neither of these conversations are of use to me right now, but I make a mental note of both of them in case they are important in the future. The screen images of the two managers discussing leather are tangible, palpable, physical, and real. If I reached out to touch them, I believe they would flinch, but, of course they won't because they are thousands of miles away. The ongoing meeting technology also has algorithms in its search functions that allow me to access all previous communications from any of the company's ongoing meetings on any subject that have occurred during the two and a half years that the network has been in existence. At first, it was a little disconcerting to realize that nothing ever goes away and everybody knows what everybody else is doing. But I soon came to understand the incredible efficiencies when communications are made so open and accessible that one can always go back and review them.

I text my sad story of likely losing this customer into the ongoing meeting, asking my boss, a senior manager, to contact me when he gets a chance. About an hour later, something very unusual happens: I received a video call from my boss outside of the ongoing meeting network. His face pops up on my virtual screen with a text below, like a foreign movie subtitle.

"Look, about this PI Furniture customer situation: don't discuss it with anyone. Mark Atkins, our CEO, wants to talk to you about this."

This was so unusual that I was stunned. "What do you mean talk to me?"

"He wants to see you in person. Go up to Chicago tomorrow and meet with him at 2:00. Here's the address. I can't really talk about this anymore."

It is late afternoon, and I am tired and want to go home to get ready for the drive to Chicago, but first I need to check in on a production job in South Africa. I point my finger at the screen to change to a different ongoing meeting, this one relating to a project involving local production of a line of glass and metallic desks for a retail chain in Johannesburg. On one corner of the virtual screen is a square, which I signal with a wave of my finger. The square opens to reveal a factory floor. I make another gesture and the factory expands so that I am surrounded by the factory, as if I am standing in the middle of the floor. I understand the technology behind this: tens of thousands of tiny camera sensors are imbedded all over the factory. By moving my body, I am able to virtually maneuver through the factory, observing the progress of the job. What I see are transparent cages enclosing robotic arms and fingers, assembling glass and metal for the desks. The glass is being transported by a mobile robotic device holding about half dozen six-foot slabs of glass. The robot removes the glass and places it in front of the stationary robotic arms, permitting the arms to begin assembling the metal parts to construct our tables. I do not see people on the factory floor, so I "move" my body to an adjacent office where the factory supervisor is sitting in front of his own virtual screen overseeing the manufacturing for not only me but for a number of other clients. I ask how it is going. He tells me that our project was proceeding as "smooth as glass," laughing at his silly joke. He assures me that it will be done in two or three days and in the retail stores within a week. I decide to take a further inspection tour. In a room off the main factory floor, I observe the glass tabletops being formed by 3D printing machines by injecting a liquid "glass" from a vat into a mold that, in effect, prints the glass for the table. With the computer assisted design technology, we can alter the shape and size of the glass tops to suit any special orders. The materials used to make the glass are synthetic so that the glass tables are impervious to chipping or cracking and are far lighter than the real glass. This is important, because the mobility of the retail customer requires home/office furniture that can easily be moved when they

Jobs of the Near Future?

relocate. One of the reasons that our company is successful is that we provide not only beautiful custom designs but extremely hardy, light, and portable furniture. After examining the glass production, I shift myself into another side room where the metal legs and braces for the tables are being produced by robots equipped with laser cutting tools that shape the parts. That the robotic and 3D computer controlled technology can be located in a factory near the customer to produce the entire table is a tremendous cost saver to us.

This is the first time I have used this particular factory, but their ratings by other companies were extremely high. When I chose them, I could see the ratings from companies that had used them for production and from the retail outlets and ultimate customers about the quality of the product. This level of transparency makes it far easier to select a manufacturing plant, vendor, or supplier. Obviously this kind of transparency cuts both ways. Negative reviews can pretty much kill a business quickly.

Our division president Bill Baxter has pushed us to use local vendors and producers, companies that are close to the ultimate customer. As a practical matter, this means using thousands of companies to produce our products. A large part of my job and the jobs of my fellow managers is to oversee this incredibly complex value chain. But it has worked extremely well for our company, because without long distance shipping we can get the product to the customers quickly with minimal shipping costs. Our boss' forceful use of virtual technology to hire, monitor, and supervise thousands of supply chain partners has helped put our company on top. He constantly tells us that in order to keep ahead of everybody else, we must have the very best technology and the most outstanding people working for us. Perhaps that's why he's been so ruthless in firing people who are not flexible about taking on any task necessary to accomplish the job.

Satisfied that things are very much under control, I close the window of the ongoing meeting for this project and move back into the ongoing meeting for our division. I ask, "Fred, are you around?" Fred is a colleague who holds the same job that I do and generally works with me on the same projects. Our bosses use a team approach so that every project has at least one manager available at all times. I intend to sign off for 10 or 12 hours, and I want to make sure that Fred is available to cover me. But he does not respond, which is odd because I've not heard from him for over a day. If anything, he is diligent to a fault, checking in even if he is off duty. I decide that I will go home anyway and periodically check in to make sure everything is under control. In an emergency, anyone can get a hold of me by sending me a beep, which registers as a noise from a tiny speaker imbedded in my left ear lobe. I rarely get beeped because Fred is very good about having my back. Of course, few people work set hours in this company. While our bosses tell us that downtime is very important, most of us are so committed and immersed in these projects that we constantly flow in and out of work. But when we need extended downtime and vacations, we can easily get it, and the company encourages it. However, if I am on vacation and I need to work, it is easy to do so with our virtual screens, which I can access anywhere. I can always enter an ongoing meeting, giving me immediate access into factories, documents, and communications. There really is no need for me to ever be in an office, and some of my co-workers have chosen to work at home. Personally, I like separating my work space from my home space, and so I maintain a separate office.

I close off my virtual meetings with a wave of my hand. The screen encompassing me disappears, revealing my physical office, an immense, brightly lit room populated by other workers at desks, some of whom are blocked from view by their own virtual screens, which do not permit anyone to observe what they are doing. But I do see many people walking around the room, chatting and joining groups in cozy couch and chair coffee areas.[107] I selected this particular office space because there are other workers in the manufacturing design business, albeit working for different companies. While there's no one from my company among the 200 or so people who work in this space, I find it stimulating and informative to chat with others who are engaged in similar occupations. Everybody in this office space works pretty much the way I do; that is, virtually. Some have four or five colleagues from their own companies in the workspace, but generally their co-workers are not part of their department.

I walk through the open space saying goodbye to various acquaintances, looking around at the views of the wetlands through the floor to ceiling windows on all four sides of the space. It's hard to believe that this building was formerly a big box store in a now obsolete shopping mall. The developers of this community retrofitted a dying working class suburb by redesigning empty mall space into modern, sustainable environments containing offices, dining, recreation, nightclubs, cultural centers, apartments, and homes.[108] While I moved into this community to be close to my parents, a lot of people have come here because it provides great quality of life. The cost of living is reasonable, there is little or no commute, and there is wonderful entertainment, dining, and recreation. In the last few years there has been a real move to "local work clusters" throughout the United States and the world. Because there is no need to go to a central office or even a regional office, developers have provided mixed use residential business communities, designed to provide a lively and convivial quality of life with comfortable, convenient

107 "Working Alone. Together," *New York Times*, 13 May 2013.
108 NPR, Ellen Dunham-Jones, "The Future of Cities, TED Radio Hour," 15 June 2012.

workspaces and accessible transportation when people want to travel. I lived in a big city when I was married and enjoyed its culture and excitement, but I really don't feel I'm giving anything up here, because just about everything available in a city is right here.

On the way home, walking through the mall, I stop for groceries and household supplies that I need but had not gotten around to picking up because I've been so busy. I walk into the Complete Store, a four level complex. I like this retail establishment because I can find just about anything I need for day-to-day life, and it gives me the option of shopping very quickly if I am in a hurry or taking my time. Because of the large size of the store, it offers a virtual instruction guide where I can simply murmur a question such as "where is the black shoe polish," into the air and immediately receive text directions on my contact lenses directing me to the floor, aisle, and section with the product. Today I am in a rush, so I simply stand at the entrance of the store, reciting my list of groceries into the air, and I wait a few minutes while robotic carts swarm at me from various points in the store carrying the items that I requested. I examine them to make sure I received what I wanted, particularly to see if the fruits and vegetables meet my high standards. Everything looks good, so I say "ok" which unleashes a robotic cart which bags the items for me. As I walk out of the story carrying the three bags, invisible sensors with recognition software identify me, charge my credit system, and instantaneously send me a receipt, which I can view on my contact lenses. I pause at the door for a moment to review the charges and then leave. The whole process takes about five minutes.

Most of the time I enjoy walking around the aisles selecting the products myself and seeing other customers. It is still a little strange not to see store clerks or checkout people. If I have inquiries about a product, I can simply ask the question into the air and receive a text answer on my contacts or, if I choose, an oral response into my implanted ear plugs. If the store is out of a product, I can voice an oral request into the air to purchase it, and it will be delivered to my condo the next day. When I order a product this way, I don't have to fill out a form because the sensors in the store recognize me and process the order. The only store employees are technicians who monitor and program the software. They walk around greeting customers as they are working from their virtual screens. There are also human waiters in the three store restaurants. When I get a meal here, the waiter will make food suggestions based on his review of my virtual recorded history of food preferences. I gave permission to restaurants to do this because I like the waiters to see my preferences in food and wine and to know my food allergies. Any restaurant can tap into the virtual record of my dining experiences. The really good waiters will suggest dishes that push me a bit out of my comfort zone, and I almost always enjoy the food because they use AI software that analyze my taste bud preferences to determine what dishes and wine I would enjoy. I have to remind myself that these waiters are really dining technicians because they rely so heavily on technology to serve the customers. I have also given permission to allow the restaurant kitchens to use my food history to slightly alter dishes on the menu to adjust for my dietary preferences; in my case, less salt and more cheese.

Leaving the Complete Store, I enter a wide street with low rise buildings and walk for 15 minutes to a group of small townhouses, where I take an escalator rising over a common garden area onto a floor leading into my 2,000 square foot residence. As I enter my home, I think about the two-week training course that Bill Baxter held for new employees at his summer residence in Maine. He talked about the culture of the company and his philosophy for reinventing the home office furniture business. He demonstrated the company's virtual technology, and we practiced by simulating ongoing meetings where we communicated with colleagues and partners all over the planet, supervising production and purchasing. Bill told us we could reside anywhere in the world we desired as long as we could get to a major airport within a few hours when it was necessary to travel. The town where I live is about a two hour drive from Chicago and has an underground train which can quickly take residents to Chicago. There are also new small, pilotless drone planes that depart from a microairport in our town. These planes can take passengers directly to any place within a 1,500 mile range. While I expected I would be doing a lot of travelling given the worldwide nature of our business, during the three years of my employment, I've taken perhaps a half dozen trips. There's simply no need to visit our customers, suppliers, and producers because the technology we use to communicate with them is so vivid and real. I have found that we communicate better virtually, particularly where there are many participants, than we do in face-to-face meetings.

Most people of my generation grew up in a virtual social world where our friendships and romances were as much through texting, social media, and video as they were face-to-face, so we are highly practiced in virtual relationships. And since all our communications in our ongoing meetings are recorded, there is far less chance of misunderstanding and miscommunication than from old-fashioned personal meetings or one-on-one teleconferences where people may forget or get confused. After growing up in a socially networked world, it has not been much of a change for me to conduct business in the same virtual way, particularly since the technological tools we have are exponentially better, faster, and clearer than the ones we used even a few years ago. Our virtual meetings are more real to me than face-to-face meetings.

Jobs of the Near Future?

One of the questions that Baxter posed at the training sessions has come back to me over and over again. He asked the group, "What is our workforce?" One person answered that it is the people who are on our payroll. Another said, "Well, I suppose it could include independent contractors." Bill said that both of these answers were incorrect. After listening to a half a dozen "wrong" responses he said, "I'll tell you who our workforce is. It is everyone in the world. Our business policy is to use the very best people anywhere to design, produce, provide materials and in any other way contribute to our product and services. Our workforce is potentially everyone." In the three years since I began working here, I've seen Baxter's policy in effect as we acquire furniture designs from complete strangers from every corner of the globe. Some of these designs have become our most successful products.

I've also seen Baxter's policy in practice as our division uses the open source approach in developing new products. For example, the glass and metal tables that we are producing in South Africa use a new lightweight metal resin alloy that a designer thought was necessary to create the look and lightness of the metal for the table. We had used a synthetic metal in a product two or three years ago, but it did not provide the appearance or the weight that we desired. So Bill said, "Let's make available to the public on our open supplier network the formula for our metal and our specific objectives of making it better and solicit input from experts elsewhere." While some were concerned that he was giving away our proprietary information, he insisted that we would gain more by going open source than we would lose in making our formula public. We did so, and an obscure hobbyist from Indonesia suggested a new synthetic metal blend that turned out to be just what we were looking for. We paid him for his efforts, which even with a generous fee and royalty was a bargain. Bill said if someone else wants to use our new formula, then "best of luck to them." His creed is that we cannot be paranoid about someone stealing our products, and if we want to close ourselves off for the sake of protecting what we own, we are cutting ourselves off from the best and brightest people in the world and the newest and best technology. So far, it's all seemed to work, because in the past three years our home furniture division has gone from being one of the pack to the undisputed leader in the industry.

At home, I glance at my combined living room/workspace, which I designed myself because I thought it would be good experience since I would be doing it with customers. During my training in Maine, Baxter had a design expert who said that recent neurobiological studies showed that workplace environment significantly affects how one thinks and works.[109] Thus ceiling height, color, type and placement of the furniture contribute to the worker's creativity, ability to focus, recall of facts, and interpersonal skills.[110] So I used my newfound design knowledge to create my own home office. One important facet of the new virtual technology is that it can be configured to one's unique working and lifestyle. Some people like to work with virtual paper, which has the look and feel of old-fashioned documents. Other workers are stimulated by a game-like virtual environment where colors, shapes, and moving objects are used to perform their work tasks. Neurological studies have shown that a game interface keeps some people focused and less subject to distraction because it activates particular neurons conducive to concentration. I like to work with a flat surface in front of me, so at home I use a large desk that converts into a virtual desk. While it may be old-fashioned to have a desk because no one uses files or paper anymore, I like a desk to display my personal items and a screen

109 Institute for the Future, "Future Work Skills 2020," (2011), www.iftf.org/futureworkskills2020.
110 Ibid., 11.

surface to design rooms for our customers.

In my home space, my virtual robotic assistant sits at her own virtual work station in the corner of the room. While I take her to the office with me most days, today I left her at home. When I walked in the door, she genuinely seemed as if she missed me, asking what happened at work and how I was feeling. Of course, I know she is a robot with artificial intelligence, but emotionally I relate to her pretty much like a real secretary. She is virtually connected with all of my ongoing meetings and knows everything that goes on in my work world. She is also a good conversationalist, and I can talk to her about my problems. I know that she is nothing more than circuits and sensors, but I must admit I have a personal relationship with her, and I like and respect her. With the falling prices of chips, sensors and cloud memory, robot assistants have become inexpensive, and almost all white-collar workers have one. Some people don't want a robot assistant in the form of a human being; rather they prefer to work with a virtual assistant reflected by a voice or text instead of a human-like form. But many workers like me enjoy having an assistant that looks and acts like a real person.

The artificial intelligence, algorithms, and memory capacity in my robotic assistant enable her to perform functions better than a real human assistant. She continually provides me a list of priority tasks which have a timetable, due dates, size, and all other conceivable information about the task at hand. She reminds me if I have overlooked something and monitors me as I am performing my work. She also knows what she doesn't know. For example, the other day she said, "I believe that the most important thing you have to do today is hire a resin supplier for the synthetic chairs you are producing on the West Coast project, but I'm not sure whether you want to stick with the old supplier because their deliveries have been erratic. You probably should do a cost benefit analysis on whether it's worth making a change or not. I am not absolutely certain that this is your top priority for the day, or whether a cash benefit analysis is worthwhile, but I can give you any of the numbers you need on other potential suppliers."

This afternoon she is going to help me with something else. I decided to learn Spanish because so many of our customers and vendors are from Latin countries, and I feel I will be more effective in my communications with them if I can speak the language. I took a bit of it in high school, so I'm not starting from scratch, and the new learning techniques are much better and more fun. Consequently, I'm making amazingly fast progress in really learning the language.

To do my Spanish lesson, I pulled up the virtual screen with my textbook, including video lectures. When I decided to take Spanish, I had to make a decision as to whether I would take a credited course through one of the top universities or take a not-for-credit massive open online course (MOOC). Since I was doing this for my own work-related knowledge base, I decided to do the open online course, which has an unlimited number of students. The lecturer is among the top Spanish professors in the world, and she is an engaging and fun person. I signal to my virtual screen, and the professor comes on and delivers a twenty minute lecture picking up from the point where I had left off. After she is finished, I have the choice of joining my social network study group—15 students like me who are businesspeople learning Spanish so that they can function more efficiently in their jobs. I really enjoy the study group because of the social interaction and business connections with likeminded individuals, but today I don't have time for them, so I tell my robotic assistant that we were going to do a half hour of tutoring. My robot is programmed to resume the tutoring at the point where I am in the lessons, and she does it in such an entertaining fashion that it really seems like I am working with a real person. We converse, and she incorporates new words and phrases into the dialogue as she gently corrects my errors and gives instruction. Of course, I know she is operating off of a complex algorithm designed to offer feedback, guide me, reinforce areas where I am weak, and teach me new words and grammar. The algorithms guide her to be emotionally sensitive to my moods and emotions as she reads my facial expressions and body language with her sensors. Consequently, she knows when I am struggling, bored, frustrated, or disengaged. If I am losing interest or having difficulty comprehending, she adjusts the tutoring technique to get me back on track. Nothing of her underlying computer technology is noticeable as we work; to the contrary, she comes across as a sympathetic but rigorous tutor.[111]

Students take virtual learning for granted now. I have talked at length with my eighth grade niece and her mom about today's classroom experience, trying to understand the revolutionary changes in education since I was in school. I now understand that the virtual lecturing is provided by the best educators in the world. For their classroom lessons, the students access their virtual instructors, who pick up precisely where the kids are in their progress in the courses so that each student has an individual study plan designed by algorithms. So, while my niece is in eighth grade, she is at a different point in her course work than her fellow students. She will not get left behind, nor will she be bored, because her course of study is precisely constructed for her.

I also understand that this big change in education has come about

111   "The Machines are Taking Over," *The New York Times*, 14 September 2012; "The Year of the MOOC," *The New York Times*, 12 November 2012; "Making Science Leap from the Page," *The New York Times*, 17 December 2011; "University Consortium to Offer Small Online Courses for Credit," *The New York Times*, 15 November 2012.

not because educators decided that virtual teaching was better (although the studies have shown that it is), but rather because of the crushing economic cost of the public education system. In 2010, public schools were spending $8 billion a year on textbooks. Now students use virtual texts ,which cost a fraction of that. For young children entering primary school who have been brought up with tablets and computers, using heavy, old-fashioned textbooks made no sense when virtual books were not only far cheaper but already familiar to these young digital natives. In addition, the administrative costs of public education, with voluminous student records, administrators, filing, and offices, was a crushing economic burden. Now with digitalized student records, educators can instantaneously access all information about any student. There is no longer a concern about student records disappearing when students move from one location to another. The new virtual recordkeeping is far more precise, as it contains every conceivable record, test, score and evaluation about each student from pre-kindergarten through the end of high school. The offices where administrators used to work have, for the most part, been eliminated.[112] Today, the cost of public education is far lower than it was ten years ago.

The public school students also have virtual tutoring much like the kind I enjoy with my robot. The tutoring is available either on their screen or through their home robots. Most of the kids like learning with a robot because they relate to it like a real person.[113] The psychological studies of learning processes have been incorporated into the tutoring software, and, with a combination of the very best virtual teachers and virtual tutoring, student educational achievement has hugely improved.

112   Saylor, 173-175, 178-179.
113   Ibid., 175-178.

While the kids can access their lectures and tutoring anytime or anyplace, they still go to school every day, but their school situation looks so much different than my traditional school experience. Instead of the old-fashioned classrooms, the kids now meet in study/social groups with educational facilitators who work with them on various subject matters. I attended my niece's "go to school night" a few months ago, where I sat in on a study group. The facilitator led a spirited discussion of *The Scarlet Letter*, engaging the students in a discussion of the structure of the book and the moral and sociological implications of the story to our contemporary society. The kids were then given virtual access to a half dozen versions of the book on film and stage so they could watch different interpretations of the story. Even though it was an eighth grade class, I found it stimulating and enjoyable, and I could see that the kids were into it as well. What a contrast to my boring classrooms, where most of my teachers droned on incessantly about some old text that I had struggled through the night before in my room.

I also liked that my niece's family was able to relocate to a rural community in Montana without any concern of depriving her of a first rate education. She has access to the best teachers in the world and the most up to date virtual texts and tutoring. And the family is able to live exactly the kind of life that they have decided is best for them. I'm also happy that, as a point of pride, my country, the United States, which had previously spent more money per student than just about any other country yet in 2011 ranked 25th in math and 17th in science,[114] has greatly improved those statistics so that our kids are now up at the top of the worldwide rankings. I don't know what the problem was before, but I think it was the absence of great, stimulating teachers for every student. That's all been turned

114 Ibid., 172.

around with the best teachers in the world providing virtual lectures and face-to-face contact at school led by psychologist educators who motivate and help students with the subject matter content.

Going back to the Spanish lesson, my robotic tutor tells me that I've had enough for today and that if I want to watch some good Spanish speaking movies, there are four by director Luis Bunuel imbedded in my virtual textbook. She tells me to check them out, as they use many of the words and phrases that we're working on. Next time, she says, she will do a tutoring session about the film that I choose.

The next morning, I wake up nervous about the meeting with the CEO. It is 5:30 a.m., and, while I had intended to take a high-speed train into Chicago, I realize that I have plenty of time to drive and decide that going by car will help take my mind off of the meeting. I do not own a car (very few people do anymore), so I pull up my virtual screen to check out rental availability for the lot a few blocks from my condo. There is a good selection, including a sexy new Mercedes two-door sports car. I decide to indulge myself. I rent the car by pointing my finger at the virtual car image on the screen before me. My credit information, embedded in a chip in my finger, is transmitted to the rental car company. The transaction takes a mere second. I then walk over to the car lot, where I position myself in front of the car while its sensors identify me as the designated renter and then unlock the door and fire up the engine.

In a few minutes, I am cruising down the not particularly crowded expressway. People rarely commute by car to work anymore. For most folks, their commute is simply a walk from their home to their local work space. People on the road these days are, for the most part, traveling for pleasure. I am enjoying the drive, weaving in and out of the lanes. With no speed limit and a good car, it is exhilarating. Unfortunately, I begin to worry again about the upcoming meeting, and, as I move from one lane to another, a soft automated voice says, "You just pulled in front of a car in the other lane." At the same time my car automatically accelerates and, in the rearview mirror, I can see the car in back slow down. The sensors in both of our vehicles had recognized the danger and alerted a cloud-based computer to instruct the cars to take corrective action, protecting us from a collision. That's why there's no speed limit anymore, as it's almost impossible to screw up. Millions of sensors are embedded in the roadways and automobiles, connected to clouds and software that take over the car's functions if the drivers get too close, lose control, or otherwise put themselves in jeopardy.

In any event, I realize that I am not concentrating on the road, so I flick on the automatic drive, lean back, admire the view, and let the car drive me to Chicago and into a parking lot next to the CEO's high-rise condominium near Michigan Avenue. While the car's automated driving features can maneuver through dense traffic, there are few cars on the Chicago streets, as most people walk or take comfortable trains. No one wants pollution clogging the air, so people try to stay out of their cars. Because there are very few corporations or industries located in the big cities these days, most people live there for the culture, restaurants, and beauty of the architecture. Corporate headquarters and old-fashioned office buildings have been converted into residential, shopping, eating, or cultural places.

A few minutes later I am on the 54th floor, softly knocking on the door of the CEO's residence. The door is opened by a distinguished gray haired gentleman, probably in his 70's. I walk into an expansive loft with a rough, wood beam ceiling and floor to ceiling windows on all four sides looking over Chicago from Lake Michigan on the east to the flat land spreading out to the west. The room contains sparse glass and chrome modernistic furniture. Sitting at a glass desk in the far corner of the room is a woman in her early 40's dressed in a severe gray suit. Speaking with an Indian accent, she introduces herself as the company's intellectual property content protection lawyer. I ask her where she is based, and she replies that she works all over.

The CEO asks me to sit. "You know we rarely have face-to-face meetings, but this is a special matter, and I suppose I'm old-fashioned, since I wanted to meet." He motions to the lawyer.

The lawyer tells me, "Bill Baxter, your boss and the division head, left the company a couple of days ago. It appears that he is setting up a rival company using the identical business model as your home furniture line. As you probably know, it is the most successful part of the company."

The CEO interjects, "It's responsible for almost all of our growth and profits over the last few years. "

"You know that customer who suddenly went missing on you—we think that Baxter solicited them and other customers."

The CEO interrupts, "We are guessing that Baxter is stealing our executives, managers, and IT people. We think he's also trying to take our proprietary information. He wants to clean us out. We have been working to develop new artificial intelligence software that will virtually design home offices and furniture based on customer lifestyle and aesthetic preferences. It will put together rooms for customers, using technology that will review their lifetime product preferences and use algorithms to select furniture and décor that hits their personal sweet spot. No company has anything like this, and Baxter is trying to walk out the door with the technology."

The lawyer looks at me. "Have you been solicited to leave?"

"No. I'm shocked. When I couldn't get a hold of the potential customer, I thought they had just changed their mind. I had no idea this was happening."

"We didn't think they had approached you because when we looked at your work activities over the last few years, you appear to be extremely independent and have made your own way through this company. That's why we wanted to talk to you to see if you could help us."

"What do you want me to do?"

"Pay attention to what's going on and sort of work as our undercover person. Maybe you can reach out to your colleagues to ask them if they've been solicited and what is happening and then provide the information to us. We need as many facts as we can get in order to go after them in court."

"I can do that."

The CEO turns to the lawyer, "As you know, all this transparency with our business social network has always made me concerned that something like this would happen. We've shared our proprietary software with our vendors, suppliers, and customers, making us a sitting duck to have our intellectual property stolen. And now that's exactly what's happened. If we had been conducting our business the old-fashioned way when we kept our secrets closely guarded, we would not be worried about having the whole company in play like this."

"You may be right, sir, but with all due respect, I don't think so. In my experience, intellectual property theft usually is done not by outsiders, but by insiders. It is your trusted colleague and head of your key division, Baxter, who's stealing from you, not some vendor, competitor, or hacker. That's how it usually happens. You shouldn't second guess yourself. The clients we have who operate in the old-fashioned, non-transparent way are the ones who are struggling to stay in business. The successful companies, big and small, are those that have moved to an open platform where most of their software is pretty much open for their partners to see and work with. The companies that are succeeding constantly improve their products and grow their sales because they are open and collaborating with their customers and partners. If someone really intends to rip off your software, they can do it by reverse engineering, even if it is completely locked down. What's given your company an edge is that your people have been innovative, flexible, and open in working with the customers in creating international supply chains to make the products more efficiently. Don't second guess yourself. The problem here is Baxter, not your business model. He's the bad guy, not your business model."

"I would like a detailed legal analysis, laying out all of the laws that may have been violated here, with a discussion of the case law authorities, a list of all of our legal options, including courts and jurisdictions where we could bring an action. I want you to include all of the relevant patent and intellectual property statutes and common law. You should make this memo detailed and specific because I can understand it. You know, I used to be general counsel of this company. Today is Tuesday. Can you have this for me by next Monday?"

"I can have it for you within an hour."

"How can you do it so fast? Have you already prepared it?"

"No, I'm going to do it right now. If you can let me use your office for about an hour, I can prepare the memo now and give it to you before I leave here."

"I want no stone left unturned—no possibility, even remote, left unexplored."

"Sir, I will give you the best and most thorough legal analysis that money can buy."

"Do you have a team of lawyers sitting around waiting to work with you on this?"

"No. This is better than a team of lawyers. It's our artificial intelligence software that can research and write the legal analysis far better than any human can. I act as a collaborator with the technology, using my judgment and experience to tweak or modify the memo. Trust me. You're getting the best legal work available."

"Well, that's what everybody says about you, and you've done a great job for us in the past."

We conclude the meeting with the CEO, the lawyer, and me setting up a private ongoing virtual meeting. With this arrangement we do not need to make plans as to when we will next talk because our communications will be continuous from this point on through our secure network. I ask the lawyer if she will be heading back to her office. She says her office is wherever she is needed, and her home is in a rural community outside of Delhi, India. Curious about the logistics of her business, I ask her where her law firm's offices are. "We don't have a central office, and our offices are wherever the best lawyers in the world are. We hire our lawyers based on what they can contribute to our clients' needs. We don't care where they live and work."

Back home, using my virtual screen, I enter into our division's ongoing meeting. Most of the executives, managers, and employees of the home office division use the meeting site to provide status reports on projects, discuss new business prospects, and seek advice from colleagues. I rewind the meeting over the past several days, looking for clues to what Baxter has been doing. I notice that communication traffic had been unusually light. There are questions posed by several managers, unanswered by anyone, and more strikingly I see no communications from any senior division managers and executives. Since it is the senior staff that typically weighs in on questions, this seems strange.

I decide I will ask for input regarding my potential customer loss. I lay out the whole story in video, then wait for responses. None come. Typically for a customer matter, particularly a retail chain, the executive team would have jumped all over this, asking questions and providing advice. But today, not a word. All day, as I work on other matters, I keep checking back to this meeting, but all is quiet.

Late in the afternoon I enter the new ongoing meeting site with the CEO and outside lawyer and report what I have observed, or rather *not* observed, during the day. I tell them that something is clearly wrong.

After dinner, I let in the plumber. I contacted her to look at a damp wall in my bedroom that I have been ignoring for the last several weeks. This plumber was recommended by a neighbor who said she was expensive but efficient and accurate. When I show her the wet wall, she puts on a pair of what appear to be Coke bottle glasses. She explains that the glasses are a kind of an MRI device designed for the construction industry. I watch as she wanders around the apartment gazing at ceilings, floors, and walls.

"You called me in the nick of time." "There is a defective pipe, and it has a slow leak that is getting bigger. The entire tubing is cracked, and it's right below this floor surface."

Alarmed, I ask, "When can you fix it? Do you have to order new parts?"

"I could pull back the floor and patch it, but that's just a temporary fix. Better to replace the entire six foot pipe. Even though it's custom designed for this space, I can go out to my truck and print a new one now." She leaves the apartment and returns in 15 minutes carrying a six foot pipe. She begins removing the old pipe and installing the new pipe.

I ask, "How did you do make it so quickly?"

"Oh, the MRI glasses contain sensors that photograph a multi-dimensional image of the broken pipe, which is transmitted to computer assisted design software and then fabricated on a 3D printer in my truck. We use a new lightweight resin for the pipe. It's virtually indestructible. It'll last a lifetime and weights almost nothing. Actually, this is really an easy job, although I must tell you, if you had brought in a regular plumber, he would have tried to order the part, found out that it's custom, and you would have waited weeks while a shop made a stainless steel pipe. In the meantime, your entire wall would have rotted out and would have had to be replaced. Anyway, the job's done."

I had been reading about the new breed of plumbers who make a six figure income, but I did not really understand their value and efficiency until today. This plumber was really a technician collaborating with her software and a portable manufacturing device. Whatever her bill was, it would be well worth it.

After the plumber leaves, I check back into the ongoing meeting with the CEO and lawyer. While there had been no live discussion between them, each had provided video discussing the situation. The stunning news from the CEO was that the entire executive team of our division had left the company, taking most of the managers and IT staff. He said there were also strong rumors that a venture capital firm was financing a new venture headed by Baxter. The CEO had dissected the legal memo provided by the lawyer and concluded that, based on a review of all similar cases brought in the appropriate jurisdictions, it was extremely unlikely that a judge would issue an injunction shutting down the new company because judges were reluctant to deprive anyone of a livelihood. The best course of action, the lawyer recommended, was to bring a lawsuit against the new company and Baxter for the value of their new business. The lawyer said her legal theory was that Baxter and the other deserters had stolen our entire home office furniture business, including the proprietary business plans, software, employees, customers, and everything else of value. Hopefully, she said, the size and scope of the lawsuit would frighten the departed employees and discourage more people from leaving.

There is a second video from the CEO telling me that I had been promoted to vice president of manufacturing, effective immediately, to replace the individual who left with Baxter. The CEO said that they had identified me as an up and comer based on my versatility in seeing the big picture and flexibility in working with customers, colleagues, and vendors. He said that while these circumstances may not be the best way to get a promotion, he would not have given me the job unless he thought I was well qualified. Otherwise they would have hired from the outside, which they will probably do for a number of the other openings created by the departures. In any event, he said he trusts me and encouraged me to move forward and try to get beyond this setback. I wondered whether this was an opportunity or burden, but I decided to take on the challenge.

The next morning, I deal with yet another personal issue. At 6:30 I take the underground solar powered tram under my building for a ten minute ride to our local medical care unit. I am going in for treatment of a chronic cartilage injury to my left knee, caused by a tennis mishap when I was a teenager. I now play a couple of times a week, but lately knee pain has sidelined me. When the knee did not improve with physical therapy, my care provider team recommended cartilage replacement surgery. That is what is scheduled for this morning.

There is no general hospital in my community. In fact, the all-purpose hospital is pretty much obsolete everywhere. Instead, there are hundreds of thousands of medical care units throughout the country, primarily designed as surgical centers, intensive care, and emergency facilities. These days people are only hospitalized for life threatening, intensive care purposes, as all other conditions can be treated and monitored at home. The traditional hospital was like a box store trying to provide all medical services to all patients, but increasingly failing to do so based on shortages of specialists. Now, with virtual communications, it is no longer necessary to have fully staffed hospitals. The same business social networks we use in our company are now also used to provide medical treatment. For my treatment, my primary care physician enlists a world famous cartilage injury specialist based in Madrid. Via virtual screen, MRI images captured at my local medical care unit are reviewed and discussed by my healthcare team. Usually, it is not even necessary for me to go to the medical care unit because nano sensors placed in my body years ago track every aspect of my health and wellbeing.[115] Consequently, my primary care physician remotely monitors my blood pressure, respiratory rate, heart rhythm, and every other vital sign to determine my health status.[116] This ongoing monitoring is

115   Ibid., 153-154.
116   Topol, 194-195.

comforting, for it can determine early onset of a heart attack, stroke, and cancer. Overall, it is comforting to know our national healthcare system is no longer reactive but proactive through these monitoring tools that begin functioning before birth with imbedded biosensors providing early warnings for medical conditions that in the past would have only been diagnosed decades later, often when it was too late to treat them.[117]

This all works for me, because I rarely need to visit a doctor because remote monitoring makes it almost unnecessary. The cartilage specialist brought in by my primary care physician has never examined me in person because he practices in Spain, where he can be close to several professional sports teams that use his services. My doctor recommended him because he was considered the best in the world for this type of knee condition. When he consented to take on my case several months ago, he was granted access to all of my medical records, which are available in a virtual vault on my personal medical network. This way he could quickly look at my medical history from birth. I still find it amazing that my physicians can instantaneously see my entire medical history, including every doctor visit, x-ray, and note, all located in a secure cloud.

The healthcare industry was the biggest laggard in converting to electronic records and virtual communications. What finally propelled it to change was the crushing cost of US healthcare, which at the beginning of the second decade of the 21st century was consuming over 17% of the US gross domestic product. At that time, most medical records were still paper files, requiring doctors to spend almost 40% of their time locating files and making handwritten observations. Where patients moved or retained a specialist, it was difficult, if not impossible, to locate and transfer all

117   Ibid., 161-168.

the applicable records. Often patients' files were incomplete, leading to medical error.[118] It was only when some hospitals and younger physicians began aggressively using available technology that healthcare became cheaper and more efficient. It was the efficiencies that forced a transformation in the practice of medicine; in effect the medical profession was coerced into become virtual.

Doctors also soon realized that by using virtual social networks to communicate and consult with one another on diagnoses and best courses of treatment, the quality of their work improved substantially. Now all doctors double-check their diagnosis by accessing a virtual bank of all of the world's medical research and knowledge. Algorithm searches designed for the medical professional serve to allow the physicians to collaborate with technology in their treatment of patients. To determine the best treatment for my cartilage injury, not only did my specialist employ his own considerable professional experience and knowledge, but he used my MRIs and other data about my condition to compare it to all worldwide treatment histories of patients with the same injury. So when I come into the medical unit today for my procedure, I am confident that I have the benefit of not only the best specialist but the most comprehensive information available in the world to determine my treatment plan. This is because the software algorithms and virtual medical research library is available to everyone all the time, and it is inexpensive because it is obtainable without travel, books, paper, or a brick and mortar infrastructure.

At the medical care unit, I am ushered into a small operating room where I am greeted by a young woman who introduces herself as the surgical professional. She explains that her job is to work with my remote surgeon and a da Vinci robotic device to perform the

118 Saylor, 145-148.

cartilage replacement procedure. She points to a machine with an octopus-like arm in the corner of the room and asks me to stretch out on an operating table in front of it. She explains that this device will implant cartilage that had been prepared by a 3D bio printer this morning. The bio printer has been directed by computer assisted design images which replicated my pre-damaged cartilage. The cartilage is made of biosynthetic material and tested to assure my body will not reject it.[119]

After prepping my leg for the procedure, the specialist appears on a virtual surround screen. After examining the setup, he says, "Let's do this thing." He uses his hands to direct the robotic arms, which instantly make laser incisions in my knee and implants the new cartilage. It is all over in less than a minute.

"We're finished, and it looks good to me. We are going to put on a lightweight knee brace that you will wear for a week. Tomorrow at 9:00, I will examine you at home. We've implanted high resolution nano sensors in your knee area, which will allow me to see and feel precisely how the healing is proceeding. If I detect any problem, I will contact you immediately and get you back in here for any corrections, but I don't anticipate that. Rest assured we will be monitoring you 24/7, and I'll talk to you tomorrow."

I stand up and gingerly walk out of the room, relieved that there is very little discomfort. Within a few minutes, I am back in my office.

Later that afternoon, Fred Malone, another supply chain manager, appears up on my virtual screen in the "personal communication" box. I am puzzled as to why he would contact me outside of the division ongoing meeting, particularly on the personal channel,

---

119 Chuck Salter, "The Doctor of the Future," *Fast Company*, 1 May 2009; "The Future of Health, Now in 3D!," *Washington Post*, 27 November 2012; Kaku, 81-83.

Jobs of the Near Future?

where the communications are not preserved. The personal channel was designed to prevent others, particularly litigants, from obtaining what are meant to be wholly personal matters. Fred's three-dimensional image materializes on the virtual screen. He congratulates me on my promotion to manufacturing VP. "I have something I want to talk to you about offline, if you've got a few minutes. You may have heard that Baxter left and has taken some people with him. I'm joining him as well."

I am upset that a good manager is leaving, but at least I can try to do the undercover investigation requested by the CEO. I ask, "Why are you leaving?"

Fred says, "You know Baxter is the visionary who is the key to success of this entire company. He got some funding from a venture capital group and is going set up his own company. I want to work with him. This company is nothing without Baxter."

"Who else is going with him?"

"Well, I can't say for sure, but I think a lot of the key talent around here has chosen to join him."

"What's the new company going to do?"

"I don't know for sure, but probably work in the same space."

"You mean home furniture design?"

"I wouldn't be surprised if that was it."

"How can he possibly compete with the economic resources that we've got? It seems to me this is a real flyer."

"Well, basically all the work we do in this division is virtual. And all the manufacturing is outside the company done by contractors. That's why they love you and me—because we know how to work the value supply chain to efficiently produce a great product and manage the customers and employees at the same time. I know Baxter would like to have you join us."

"Are you authorized to make me an offer?"

"No. I'm just feeling you out on my own because I know how good you are, and you'd be happy in this new venture. I am guessing that they will give you much more money."

"Well, let me think about it and I'll get back to you."

I report all of this back to the CEO and lawyer, who tell me they are grateful for my loyalty.

In the end, I stay with my company, but I watch as almost all our talented people leave for Baxter's new company, which opens for business several months later, offering home office furniture in direct competition with us. The new company goes public in less than a year and quickly achieves a market valuation of 10 billion. Our lawyer files a lawsuit against Baxter's company, seeking the full value of the new company for damages. Our legal theory is that Baxter has effectively stolen our company by taking our employees, trade secrets, business plan, patents, and customers. Our lawyer says the evidence showing Baxter's misconduct is very strong.

A year later, the case is settled, with Baxter paying our company $750 million to resolve the case. As it turns out, the payment does not slow down Baxter's company's growth. Within three years, his company dominates the industry, and our market share dwindles to a fraction of what it had been.

Last week, we were notified that our management had accepted an offer to sell our entire company to Baxter. After the acquisition closes, I will report to Baxter as the vice president of manufacturing.

Baxter contacted me last week on the new ongoing meeting channel between the two companies to facilitate the logistics of the merger. He said that one of the reasons he bought the company was that he wanted me on his team. "Continued success in business is not just about the software or the product or the resources," he tells me. "It's about the people."

CHAPTER 5
What You Can Do to Get Ready

We are about to enter a new work world where flexible, adaptive attitudes and thinking are the core attributes for success as a worker. Change is already happening: the evaporation of those jobs that require the employee to show up every day and perform the same tasks over and over again. Whether it's the blue-collar worker on the factory line or the manager shuffling papers, these routine jobs are disappearing.[120] At the same time, we are seeing increasing job opportunities where people need to think, reason, analyze, and perform a variety of tasks outside of their normal job description. These include higher paying jobs in managerial, technical, and professional positions, as well as lower paying service positions.[121] Soon we will encounter a tipping point where all jobs will require the worker to collaborate with new supercharged robust technology while using social/business virtual networks to continually communicate with colleagues and customers. The need for every worker to use adaptive thinking will be essential for survival in the new work environment. Yet the attributes that I see in so many working people over the age of 40 are the exact opposite of what they will need. Individuals who have performed the same job for 20, 30, or 40 years tend to have the belief that "this is the way my work should be done." They reject new ideas or prophecies of change. Not only

120 David Autor, "The Polarization of Job Opportunities in the US Labor Market," The Center for American Progress and The Hamilton Project, April, 2010, economics.mit.edu/files/5554; Institute for the Future.
121 Autor; Institute for the Future.

do they resist the notion that change is coming, but they reject the possibility that they should consider altering the way they work.

This attitude is expressed in many ways:

"I get so many emails that I can't keep up with them. Why don't people simply call me? It is a much better way to conduct business."

"We want our employees to be at their desk working where we can see them at 8:30 a.m. every morning. We do not believe in this idea of remote work."

"I need to have all my work printed on paper where I can see it, feel it, mark on it, and make revisions. Anyone who provides a memo or report to me must give it to me in paper form."

"I am not interested in learning the new software that my firm is installing. My boss tells me that I am doing a great job. I don't need to waste my time learning technical stuff that I don't need."

"I have always performed my day-to-day job alone, without collaborating with colleagues. I work very efficiently this way, and I don't understand why it would benefit me or the company to work in teams. I think it would be a waste of time."

"My boss, who is the head of our company's [marketing, human resources, sales, or manufacturing] does not know what social networking is, and cannot imagine why it would have any relevance to our jobs or company."

"I don't like to share information about my work with colleagues. When I do so, it is only on an as needed basis. I will not change because it is the best way to work."

"I express myself best through face-to-face communications. I have difficulty articulating my thoughts, ideas, and emotions on a business subject in emails or text. This is not a problem because the important business dealings are done face-to-face, and that will never change."

"I only feel truly comfortable dealing with the people who come from the same socio-economic background that I do. Truthfully, I really don't think it's important for my career to be able to relate to people in different cultures or countries because they are not really part of my company."

"I am really not a people person, but it's never mattered, because I have a total mastery of my job and can perform it better than anybody else. I don't really need to be able to schmooze with colleagues and outside suppliers to effectively do my work, and I don't plan to change at this point in my career."

"The truth is I really hate all of this technology. It's for the young people, not me. I have so much experience, wisdom, and judgment that I bring to my job. These young people who are whizzes at technology don't have the experience to take over my job."

In conducting the research for this book, I have heard these views expressed by brilliant leaders of some of the most successful organizations in the world and by retail sales people. The common denominator among the people holding these attitudes is that they are over the age of 40. It seems that the older the person, the less open they are to change. Younger people, those who are digital natives, almost never express such views. While most of them respected their senior colleagues and superiors, almost all of them told me that they thought they were dinosaurs.

If you fall into the category of people who think that nothing new is going to happen in the work world but are now beginning to sense that "the times they are a-changing," it is time to change your attitude. Without a personal recognition that things will or at least might change in a way that will affect your job and ability to make a living, you will not be able to adapt to the new work world. Think about what I have said in this book about the changes that are coming and start paying attention to the media for information about what is happening right now. Every single day, there is a news story that in some small or large way evidences what I am saying in this book. Once you start to really open your mind, you will be ready to take some concrete steps to prepare yourself. This chapter discusses some of the things you can start to do right now.

1. USE SOCIAL NETWORKS

One of the big points I hope you've taken from this book is that we will work in a world where we are continually connected to our business colleagues, customers, and partners. This is because collective information will be the key to getting things done in the work world. The old adage "no man is an island" will be the most important truism in your work life. If you lack the ability to connect with others, to share and obtain information, and communicate your intentions and ideas, you will be obsolete. If you are skeptical that this will happen in the near future, consider the Arab Spring. In Egypt, not only was social media (Facebook, Twitter, etc.) the communication means by which the revolution was accomplished, but, more tellingly, the Internet users who led the revolution were predominately young men. Even though only 21% of Egyptians used the Internet, they were almost all young people. [122] If social networking can provide the technological foundation for a political upheaval, it can and will have the same revolutionary impact on the working world.

122 Rainie and Wellman, 207.

Recently, a group of experts studying future work skills concluded: "Connective technologies make it easier than ever to work, share ideas and be productive despite physical separation. But, the virtual work environment also demands <u>a new set of competencies</u>."[123] So, how do you gain these competencies?

Training is essential to gaining any new skill, and one of the best ways to learn to use connective technologies is to become an avid participant in social networking. Whether it's Facebook, Twitter, or whatever new format becomes available, it is the ability to communicate virtually on a continual basis that will provide you a core competency in being successful in the new working world.

Social networking will be the mother of future business networking. When I talk about using social networking, I do not mean being a passive observer on Facebook simply watching what your friends and family are saying and doing. You must be an active participant, and in this way you can train yourself.

It is important to have good technological tools; that is, a fast and stable Internet connection and a mobile device (tablet or smartphone). The process must be active, ongoing, and mobile. Be proactive in seeking out friends and contacts on your networks. LinkedIn, the business network, is a good vehicle to expand your work contacts and receive and communicate information. If you have a special interest such as a hobby or medical concern, seek out a social networking site that allows you to share and communicate with like-minded individuals. You must share information about yourself, and, to the extent you can, aid and help other people. If you do not know how to locate people or groups who are interested in your issues, learn how to find them. Push yourself to explore.

123 Institute for the Future.

As you begin to engage in social networking, learn and practice how to communicate effectively. There is a different language for virtual communications created by digital natives. It is not difficult to master, but it requires attention and exercise. It is more than simply learning the acronyms; it is mastering the context and subtext. For example, communications via Facebook carry a different connotation than a text message. Look at how people communicate and the emotional context of what they are conveying. If you write a sentence that seems terse and severe, learn how to soften it. In social networking, people learn how to say more with less. You will need to acquire these skills.

Learn how to act appropriately for the social media you are using. Just as in real life interactions we modify our behavior according to the situation, we must do the same in social media communication. You have seen the problem with an individual who does not know how to write a proper email and offends where he intends to instruct, or amuses where he intends to be serious, or uses the wrong acronyms. You do not want to be the person who thought that LOL means "lots of love" as opposed to "laughing out loud" or does not realize that using all capital letters is yelling. The only way to master this new language is to practice.[124]

In addition, you should understand that your communications on any social media platform will be available to the world. People over 40 have a very difficult time internalizing this because they have grown up in a world where face-to-face verbal or telephone communications disappear immediately. Mitt Romney made highly damaging statements during his presidential campaign in a private meeting because he lacked an implicit understanding that phone video is almost always used when a celebrity speaks, and that words and conduct never disappear. By becoming proficient on

124 "The Emily Posts of the Digital Age," *New York Times*, 29 March 2013.

social media, you can learn these lessons before you begin working in a business network environment, where your mistakes can have serious, permanent, adverse ramifications on you and your business.

Part of the competency you must develop is how to understand graphic language. That means the ability to look at graphics on a screen and be able to interpret them.[125] Competency in navigating Internet "geography," hyperlinks, network information, research tools, and other graphic tools is part of this knowledge base. This is not only essential for understanding what you are looking at on a screen in the virtual world, but it is also necessary for you to obtain information. We have all seen colleagues look for information online where one person will quickly hit a dead end while another obtains a treasure trove of valuable information. The successful researcher has graphic literacy, and it is an essential skill that you need to master.

As you practice social networking, you should also try to develop what some experts call "context and connection literacy"—a skill that involves sifting through a mass of information and deciding what is important or reliable and what isn't.[126] For example, if you are part of an online chat group involving a particular medical condition, your ability to judge which sources are reliable is an important skill. Successful use of social media involves the capacity to review information from media sources, friends, and acquaintances for relevance, accuracy and reliability.[127]

Practicing with social media will also help you learn how to reveal or not reveal information about yourself. In the virtual business network, you will have unprecedented control over how you are viewed. You will become your own public relations manager. You

125 Rainie and Wellman, 272.
126 Ibid., 273.
127 Ibid., 274.

may attend a meeting where you are not at your mental best or are having a bad hair day. In the virtual world you can control what you say and the way you are viewed. Social networking will allow you to practice this. You will want to reveal the real you, but emphasize those aspects of yourself that are necessary and useful for the particular work communication context.

For those of you who are managers and leaders of teams, departments, or organizations or aspire to such a job, in the new work world you will lead a virtual team. The strategies for communicating with a virtual group, which may include employees, suppliers, and partners, will require the same skills you will acquire from social networking. For practice, you should consider participating in virtual worlds such as Second Life. These are online communities that participate in global gaming involving avatars that create a virtual experience.[128] While for many people the idea of online gaming has no attraction whatsoever, you would benefit from the gaming experience in the new work world.[129]

Studies by the Pew Research Center found that the most active users of technology had a bigger and more diverse network of friends and acquaintances, as well as an active virtual social life, than those who were not active users.[130] If active social networking broadens and expands your personal contacts and relationships, it will help you with your work relationships. Knowing how to connect and establish virtual rapport and effective communications with work colleagues, clients, customers and partners will be a key to success.

---

128 Institute for the Future,12.

129 Researchers at Stanford's Virtual Interaction Lab report that the personal experience with social networking and gaming provides socio-economic benefits which have a positive effect in work. As cited in *Future Work Skills*, 12.

130 Rainie and Wellman, 264.

What You Can Do to Get Ready

2. DEVELOPING MULTIPLE JOB SKILLS

As our supply chain manager in Chapter Four showed, possessing talents and skills in a number of disciplines is an essential competency in the virtual work world. Experts studying future work skills stated it perfectly, saying,

> The ideal worker of the next decade is 'T-shaped'—they bring deep understanding of at least one field, but have the capacity to converse in the language of a broader range of disciplines. This requires a sense of curiosity and a willingness to go on learning far beyond the years of formal education. As extended lifespans promote multiple careers and exposures to more industries and disciplines, it will be particularly important for workers to develop this T-shaped quality.[131]

The time of the specialist who does only one thing well is over. To survive in the virtual work world, one must have not only a core expertise, but one must also be knowledgeable in many other areas.

The real lesson is that you must start stretching yourself right now in your job. The phrase "It's not my job" should be stricken from your consciousness. Everything and anything related to your job should be proactively embraced by you, not just when you are asked to do something else. And this is true whether you are an employee with a large corporation, an independent contractor, or an entrepreneur.

My interview with a young professional in the fashion industry illustrates how young people are doing this now. Freida was the fashion director for an online retailer, where she was in charge of high fashion women's clothing. She subsequently left the job to go out on her own. During our interview, she dispassionately rattled off

131 Institute for the Future, 11.

her current assignments, jobs, and projects. In the past year, among other things, she has been the designer of her own fashion line, now available in retail stores across the country and online. She is also consulting for a large retail fashion company. At the same time, she is assisting a software company in implementing its new electronic fashion order forms. In the course of doing all of these jobs, she designs, works with manufacturers, deals with software products, provides advice, sells, and acts as a spokesperson and PR consultant. She is a good example of the new trans-disciplinary worker, using her core expertise in fashion retailing to work in a number of related disciplines and functions.

The jobs of the near future will require a broad range of skills. A recent UK study that asked over 500 experts and consultants from around the world to compile a list of jobs of the future revealed that many, if not all, of these jobs would require numerous competencies.[132] For example, the "body part maker" will make tissue, cartilage, organ, limb, joints, skin, and flesh and muscle replacements, synthetic or regenerated from tissue or a combination thereof, using advances in bio tissues, robotics, and synthetic materials to create the replacement parts. To perform this job, the worker must have varied skillset: she will use computer aided design to create the design for the part; a biochemical background to work with tissues; and while she might spend much of the day in a laboratory or at a computer to design and produce the parts, she will also use virtual communications to confer with surgeons, other consultants, and patients.[133]

132 The list of future jobs was compiled from a survey of experts and consultants from 58 countries on six continents with approximately 500 participants. Rohit Talwar and Tim Hancock, Fast Future Research, "The Shape of Jobs to Come, Possible New Careers Emerging from Advances in Science and Technology (2010-2030)", Final Report (January 2010), U.K. Department for Business Innovation and Skills, fastfuture.com/wp .../01/ FastFuture-Shapeofjobstocome-FullReport1.pdf.
133 Talwar and Hancock.

What this means is you must constantly stretch yourself, seeking new responsibilities and assignments in your work that are beyond your normal job description. This will be discussed more in the next sections.

3. GET YOURSELF ORGANIZED

Being organized and prioritizing your tasks has always been an important component of success, but in the new virtual work world it will become an absolute necessity in order to survive. With the new social/business networking, every moment of your workday will be completely transparent and observable by your colleagues and superiors. If you are not working, they will know it. More importantly, they will know what you are working on and how much you are achieving. You will be part of an ongoing meeting, much like a Facebook network, where everything you do will be observable. High maintenance employees who require constant supervision to make sure they are on task will lose their jobs. In the past, employees could hide but still succeed despite their own disorganization and inefficiencies. Those days will soon be over.

As a first step, start assessing what you have accomplished in your job each day as if you are an invisible boss who can observe everything you're doing. Then be brutally honest with yourself as to what you have accomplished. Have you worked on the matters that really are the most important and of the highest priority? And what have you accomplished in those tasks? Was the 90-minute face-to-face conversation with your colleague at his desk productive? Did it really accomplish anything of value? Was the satisfaction you felt about the three-hour business meeting, which included an hour of preparation and an hour after to prepare notes, justified? If your boss had observed your day, would she recognize, without any explanation by you, that you added value to the project? Or would you have to try to explain to her why what you were doing was useful?

With the current telecommunication technology, home workers have little or no supervision. This is why Yahoo banned telecommunications in 2013—their employees were taking advantage of not having a boss physically present to oversee their activities. But the coming virtual work environment will not be like the current unsupervised "telecommunications" but instead will provide technology where there will be no place to hide and your contribution to the company will be far more transparent than any type of past work environment. In the Industrial Age, even if a boss was personally observing you on a factory production line, he could not see you every moment. With ongoing virtual meetings in the coming work world, all of your activities will be observable in real time and will be recorded so they can be reviewed by your employer anytime. So ask whether you are kidding yourself as to whether you are really productive. You do not need an outside expert to tell you whether you are functioning at a high level or not—you can answer the question yourself. Then, most importantly, practice being more productive.

4. LEARN HOW TO EXPAND YOUR JOB KNOWLEDGE THROUGH CYBERSPACE TOOLS

Currently there is an extraordinary amount of information applicable to your job that is available through online research tools, and, in the near future, all knowledge, including every book, article, and research paper ever written, will be available to you instantaneously. Knowing how to access and process relevant information will be a critical job tool. It is necessary for you to begin practicing now.

This means more than simply engaging in a superficial Google search or looking something up on Wikipedia. You should challenge yourself to find material information for your job every day. That is what young people do. All of their lives they have honed the necessary skills to do it. The goal for you is to expand your skills through practice and ask for help as to how to navigate and locate information.

The ability to obtain information will mean far more than a worker simply referencing research in a business memo. With the extraordinary computer power and infinite knowledge available, successful people will, in effect, fill in the gaps in their education to learn and relearn new skills and information. As a result, they will contribute much more than they can in the current work world. Since you will be presenting yourself in virtual form, you will effectively control and create the virtual person you see. Consider, for example, a colleague who may be an expert in a certain type of engineering. When he attends a meeting or participates in a project, he displays his knowledge and skill level, and that determines the scope of his participation. What you see is what you get. However, in the virtual work world, an individual's core expertise can be supplemented with knowledge and expertise from other areas and disciplines. So our hypothetical engineer, using his skill to access information from an infinite cyberspace library, can present himself as an expert in an entire range of engineering type disciplines. He is no longer the guy you go to for a specific, limited type of project; he is now a renaissance man, because he can do anything in his field. Individuals who learn to do this will be the winners, and those who limit themselves to their core expertise will be the losers. For example, while a human resource manager for an international company may have only one language, effective use of technological tools will enable her to add to her language skills using technology's ability to instantaneously translate foreign languages. By mastering the translation software, she can overcome her limitations in foreign languages and broaden her scope of responsibilities to handle HR matters globally instead of just domestically.

So in this virtual world, there are no restrictions on what you can "know" other than your own inability to obtain the information and use it. Employees with physical disabilities (hearing, sight or mobility) will be unshackled from any physical limitations because in a virtual world, physical constraints can be overcome by digital tools.

It may also be useful to you to gain a basic understanding of programming. More and more, human resource departments are looking at applicants who have some fundamental familiarity with software programs, statistical analysis, and quantitative reasoning skills.[134] This does not mean that you need to learn how to become a programmer, but if you have any aptitude or interest in understanding programming tools, it will enhance your job market value.

In the new work world, you will have access to immeasurable amounts of data and information, which can potentially be a burden instead of an asset. It will be necessary to be rigorous in filtering, prioritizing and analyzing that information and applying it to your job. One expert study identifies the skill of "cognitive load management"—turning the massive flow of information to your advantage while continuing to focus on what is important in your job.[135] Workers will have powerful technological assistance in organizing the massive information. There will be algorithm programs expressed through robotic assistants who will filter and organize information, suggest priorities in your work schedule, and

134 Institute for the Future, 10.
135 Ibid., 12.

provide every conceivable work related assistance. But even with this assistance, you will need to practice sorting out information flow so that when you conduct a Google or other work-related research, you can focus on developing your skills in sifting through the information and work on developing your own competence in managing information overload.

Perhaps the most important lesson here is not to be complacent because you have an expertise that has served you well during your career. In the new work world, information will be cheap, so your area of expertise will be readily available to others. And while you may think your long, successful experience in your job will protect you, that same experience will be rapidly gained by younger people with the aid of a vast cyberspace information bank. So begin now and challenge yourself to tap into that virtual resource and open your mind to doing whatever it takes to get the job done.

5. IMPROVE YOUR INTERPERSONAL SKILLS

One of the dichotomies of the coming virtual work world is that, while individuals will be physically working alone much more than today, they will also be more connected with their colleagues than ever before. The ongoing meeting will provide a continuous 24/7 connection among work teams through live and recorded video, text and graphics. Your ability to virtually communicate effectively will be essential to your success or failure in your job. Individuals with strong interpersonal skills that enable them to adapt to the virtual world so they can effectively articulate facts and opinion and reveal a likable personality will prosper. Those who are unable to do this will fail. Consider the current work world, where some of your colleagues come across as dynamic and vibrant in email communications, while others convey no sense of their personality and send terse, uninteresting emails. We all know individuals (you may be one) who are very effective in a face-to-face meeting but essentially disappear when they send emails. In the new virtual world, you may never personally meet the individuals you are dealing with. It is essential that you learn to fully express your personality as well as your content in the short, contained formats that comprise virtual communications. For example, preparing a short video where an individual makes suggestions on a corporate accounting issue to her colleagues requires a different communication skillset than discussing these issues in an old-fashioned face-to-face meeting or a paper memo. In the video, the sender must succinctly articulate her views in an engaging manner and provide visuals such as graphics, documents, and charts that dynamically illustrate them. Importantly, while the individual must clearly articulate facts and opinions, he must also show charm, diplomacy and likeability in this virtual communication media.

Knowing how to express your personality in virtual communications will be a critical work skill. One interviewee for this book, who worked for a Fortune 50 company, told me about managers who were unable to express the appropriate tone, attitude and diplomacy when they virtually dealt with their subordinates and colleagues in the new 24/7 work world. Oftentimes bosses would contact subordinates at dinnertime or in the evening, using an abrupt or inappropriate tone. Their supervisors realized that this was offensive and counterproductive. While they were otherwise excellent employees and could have a curt personality in an office environment without causing a problem, they were now failing because they did not know how to communicate in a virtual 24/7 world. The old-style gruff manager has no place in this world. In a world where business, family, and social life will take place simultaneously, strong interpersonal skills will be an absolute necessity.

Healthcare providers, particularly doctors, must also become adapt in virtual communications. Physicians for the most part have resisted email communications with patients, but that will change as efficiencies and economics force healthcare services into a virtual world. When patients have full and complete access to all of their medical records and information about their condition, they will demand more ongoing communication with their physicians than today's periodic, short office visits and telephone calls. The business/social networks that I have described will be put in place for the medical field so a patient will have a continuous meeting stream with her healthcare team (doctors, paraprofessionals, and support staff) and full access to all records and information on a virtual screen. There will be easy-to-understand graphics providing perpetual monitoring of the patient's condition such as cardiac arrhythmia or blood sugar for a diabetic. Possessing the skill to engage in virtual dialogue with patients will be an essential job skill for healthcare professionals.[136]

To get ready, you must begin practicing your virtual communication skills. Study emails of colleagues and friends who effectively use the media to express their personalities, thoughts, and opinions. Work on composing emails that are short, focused, and clear but also contain humor and other emotional content.

You will see, if you haven't already, that some people use numerous social media platforms to present ideas and content. For example, an individual's Tweet may contain a link to a YouTube video containing three minutes of that individual demonstrating cooking an omelet, as well as another link to her blog discussing cooking. Individuals now have their own YouTube channels where they post videos of their opinions or experiences. Proficient users of social media constantly

136 Topol, 188-191.

switch between platforms using the most appropriate one to express themselves in video, text, pictures, or graphics. This is a window into what will soon happen in the business world. Experts identify new media literacy as a core job skill for the near future workforce, noting that "user-generated media including the videos, blogs, and podcasts that now dominate our social lives will be fully felt in workplaces in the next decade."[137]

The ability to create and present on various social media platforms to engage and persuade audiences will be a necessary job skill. But when I talk to middle-aged people, many are wholly oblivious to social media. When social media communications dominate the business world, which will happen soon, these people will be in trouble. Fortunately, these social media tools are not difficult to use. The only thing that will prevent you from mastering them is a negative attitude and a reluctance to apply yourself. And you will find that there are unintended short term benefits as you expand and enrich your social connections. I am not advising you to do this because it is simply fun or enriching to your personal life; rather, you must do it because it is critical to your livelihood. So practice, push yourself and get ready.

6. BE PROACTIVE IN LEARNING NEW TECHNOLOGY

Be the first in line for every new technological tool that is available to perform your job. When your employer makes new software available for your office computer, be proactive, enthusiastic, and diligent in learning and adapting to the tools.

In my world of the large law firm, I have seen the legal assistant job transform from working for only one lawyer to having two,

---

137 Institute for the Future.

---

three, four or more bosses. The secretaries who were unable to adjust to handling a group of attorneys as opposed to one boss lost their jobs. The secretaries who succeeded were enthusiastic about learning every new software program that became available. I saw an excellent executive secretary of a powerful senior partner who never bothered to learn Microsoft Word because she was proficient with the older software. Subsequently, when her law firm merged with another firm that only used Word, she was unable to adapt. Her boss had enabled her, telling her that "she was a great secretary" and "did not need to worry about wasting her time training for software upgrades." After the merger, she was so far behind on the technology learning curve that she had to leave the firm. Other legal secretaries tried to hide their deficiencies as new technological tools became available, but eventually it became clear that they could not work efficiently enough to support three or four lawyers. My secretary told me that it required a lot of skill and effort to master the technological tools to make a complex table of contents, and many secretaries did not try to learn, continuing to manually type up the tables. When they began to receive triple assignments, they said they did not have time to take on additional lawyers because they were "too busy." The secretaries who kept up with the technology were highly productive and could easily handle four or more lawyers.

This inability to adapt and grow is, unfortunately, most often evident with middle-aged employees who falsely believe that their experience and judgment are so important to the organization that they do not need to be proficient with new technology. Some are already falling by the wayside. When the tipping point occurs in the next few years as we move into a virtual work world, those who have not adapted and have not shown a proactive attitude to learning will be underemployed or unemployed.

7. DEVELOP A DIVERSE SOCIAL GROUP

A non-discriminatory attitude and mindset will be a necessity to be successful in a virtual work world. The ability and desire to work with people who are different in race, nationality, age, socio-economic background and gender is of critical importance because your work world will be populated by every type of person. You will work in a global environment where you must relate and appreciate all of your colleagues, superiors, subordinates, partners, and customers.

A recent study deemed cross-cultural competency to be a critical future job skill because highly diverse groups will populate the business world. Studies show that groups comprised of people with a range of skill levels and perspectives outperform homogenous groups.[138] Consequently, many corporations have moved beyond believing that workforce diversity is necessary only to avoid lawsuits; now they recognize that workforce diversity is essential to success in the global business world.

What does this mean to you? It means that you must to get over any imbedded prejudices that one group is better than your own. It means that you should reach out and expand your social circle to include people who are different than you are. If you do so, one side benefit is that you will begin to appreciate that your social life is richer when you have a varied, diverse group of friends.

Personal alliances and friendships have always been important to professional success, and this will not change in the new virtual work world. People will still connect with one another and form bonds. When your work team is made up of people from all over the world—of every race, nationality, culture, and age—any personal reluctance to form friendships with them will be detrimental to you.

138 Ibid.

Start by reaching out to folks who are different from you now.

8. FINAL THOUGHTS

I know some readers have reached this point in the book and are still skeptical that significant changes will ever occur in the workplace. But it is going to happen; in fact it is quietly occurring right now. Your first ongoing business meeting site may be on your desktop computer screen or laptop instead of on a virtual surround screen. Your first robotic assistant may be in the form of an improved Siri voice assistant that functions as a support tool designed for your industry or profession. The death of the corporate central and regional office will not happen tomorrow, but it will happen, and it is already occurring as more and more as workers, with or without the permission of their bosses, are working away from a traditional office. The virtual work world that I described in this book may seem like science fiction to some, but to others, it is already the way they work.

Some readers will conclude that even if these changes come, they will not be able to change sufficiently to work in such a different way. They will say "I'm not flexible or smart enough to alter the way I've worked for 20, 30, or 40 years." But the message of this book is that you can do it. That you have read this book and made it to the end reflects that you are an intelligent and motivated person. For you and me and most of us, the biggest obstacle to change is not intelligence or age but denial and excuse. There is no doubt that you can adapt, be more successful, and have a happier, fuller and freer life in the future—just look around at what is happening in your work world and start to get ready today.

Source Notes

The notes are for the most part self-explanatory. When possible, I have identified interviewees by name. In many cases, interviewees expressed concern about the ramifications of their interviews on their business relationships. Consequently, for purposes of obtaining unfettered opinions and unvarnished facts, most of the interview subjects in this book are not identified by their real names.

Acknowledgements

I am profoundly indebted to a number of people who contributed to this book. My friend and longtime assistant Vi Rozmarek expertly typed and retyped the entire manuscript with unfailing good cheer.

My son, Todd Carey, provided insights on the use of social media in the entertainment business that opened my eyes to the profound ramifications of social media to the entire work world.

Mitch Tuchman, my friend and cousin, provided insight and ideas from his career as a Silicon Valley entrepreneur that permeate the book.

Steve Milovich, the senior human resources executive at ABC (The Walt Disney Company), showed me that there are at least some executives who understand and foresee the big changes that technology and social media will bring to the business world.

Bob Reynolds, a world class saxophonist, patiently described the effect of social media in creating a new business model.

Rakesh Madhava, CEO of Nextpoint, lent his expertise on technology in the legal profession. Carl Stern, former CEO of The Boston Consulting Group and currently Vice Chair, Investment Banking Goldman Saks, and Ed Nowak, a senior lawyer with The Walt Disney Company, both provided insight on the challenges of new technology in the legal field.

Sheldon Dorenfest gave his perspective on technology in the international business sphere.

I would also like to thank Michael Feiner, former professor of management at Columbia Graduate School of Business and former Senior Vice President and Chief People Officer for Pepsi Cola; and

Dan Lewis, director of New Media Communications and Social Media at Sesame Street; Richard and Deborah Nemisi for their insight on the changes at IBM; David Allen, chairman of David Allen Company, a productivity consulting firm; Mary Gelber; Allison Deneen; Kathy Glass for her insights on education; Kate Ciepluch; Claire Keefe; Jeannil Boji; Gail Kalinich; and Stacey Rosen.

Finally, last but certainly not least, my wife and best friend, Tina, for her patience and support during two and a half years of living with me as I obsessed and toiled over this project.

Works Cited

Acohido, Byron. "Social Media Tools Can Boost Productivity," *USA Today*, 12 August 2012.

Anderson, Chris. *Makers: The New Industrial Revolution* (Crown Business, 2012).

Autor, David. "The Polarization of Job Opportunities in the US Labor Market," Center for American Progress and the Hamilton Project, April 2010.

"The Polarization of Job Opportunities in the US Labor Market," The Center for American Progress and The Hamilton Project, April, 2010, economics.mit.edu/files/5554.

Basulto, Dominic. "The Future of Health, Now in 3D!," *Washington Post*, 27 November 2012.

Brynjolfsson, Erik and McAfee, Andrew. *Race Against the Machine* (Digital Frontier Press, 2011).

Bullinga, Marcel. "Welcome to the Future Cloud," *Future Tech* 2012, Loc. 4465.

Bureau of Economic Analysis, *Industry Economic Accounts*, 2011.

Bureau of Labor Statistics, 1997.

Bureau of Labor Statistics, 2012.

Caldow, Janet. "Working Outside the Box: A Study in the Growing Momentum in Telework," 21 January 2009, www.ibm.com/industries/government/ieg/...working-outside-the-box.pdf.

CEO.com. "Twitter, LinkedIn Emerge as Top Social Channels for Business Leaders," August 7 2013, www.domo.com/news/press-releases/new-CEO-Study-twitter.

Chen, Brian X. "Smartphones Become Life's Remote Control," *New York Times*, 11 January 2013.

Coyne, Tom. "Notre Dame Says Story About TE'O Girlfriend Dying Apparently a Hoax," *Calgary Herald*, 17 January 2013.

Davidson, Cathy N. "How IBM is Changing Its HR Game," *Harvard Business Review*, 18 August 2011, http://blogs.hbr.org/cs/2011/08/how-ibm-is-changing-hr-game.html.

Dunham-Jones, Ellen. "The Future of Cities", *TED Radio Hour*, 15 June 2012.

Eaton, Kit. "Apps That Present Highlights of the World in Front of You," *New York Times*, 20 June 2012.

Eisenberg, Anne. "Making Science Leap from the Page," *New York Times*, 17 December 2011.

Ford, Martin. *The Lights in the Tunnel, Accelerating Technology and the Economy of the Future* (Acculant Publishing, 2009).

Grossman, Wendy M. "So Why Did Microsoft Buy Skype?," *Guardian*, 12 May 2011.

Hardy, Quentin. "SAP's Marketplace Dream," *New York Times*, 2 November 2012.

"A Strange Computer Promises Great Speed," *New York Times*, 21 March 2013.

"Google Buys a Quantum Computer," *New York Times*, 16 May 2013.

Harris, Jim. *Blindsided* (Capstone, 2002).

Hart, Brad. "Will 3D Printing Change the World?," *Forbes*, 6 March 2012.

Institute for the Future. "Future Work Skills 2020," 2011, www.iftf.org/futureworkskills2020.

Jeff Jarvis. *Public Parts* (Simon & Schuster, 2011).

Jorgenson, Dale W., Ho, Mun S. and Stiroh, Kevin J. "Will the US Productivity Resurgence Continue?" Federal Reserve Bank of New York, Vol. 10, No. 13, December 2004.

"A Retrospective Look at the US Productivity Growth Resurgence," *Journal of Economic Perspectives*, Vol. 22, No. 1, Winter 2008.

Kaku, Michio. *Physics of the Future: How Science Will Shape Human Destiny and Our Daily Lives by the Year 2100* (Doubleday, 2011).

Kurzweil, Ray. *The Singularity Is Near: When Humans Transcend Biology* (Penguin Books, 2005).

Landow, George P. "The Industrial Revolution: A Timetable."

Lewis, Michael. *Money Ball: The Art of Winning an Unfair Game* (W.W. Norton & Company, Inc., 2003).

Lohr, Steve. "Tech's New Wave, Driven by Data," *New York Times*, 9 September 2012.

Manjoo, Farhad. "Will Robots Steal Your Job," Slate.com, 2011.

Manyika, James and Roxburgh, Charles. "The Great Transformer: The Impact of the Internet on Economic Growth and Prosperity," *McKinsey Global Institute*, 11 October 2011, www.iei./iu.se.

Markoff, John. "New Storage Device is Very Small at Twelve Atoms," *New York Times*, 12 January 2012.

"Skilled Work, Without the Worker," *New York Times*, 18 August 2012.

"IBM Reports Nanotube Chip Breakthrough," *New York Times*, 28 October 2012.

"Drivers With Hands Full Get a Backup: The Car," *New York Times*, 12 January 2013.

"Modest Debut of Atlas May Foreshadow Age of 'Robo Sapiens'," *New York Times*, 11 July 2013.

Marsh, Peter. *The New Industrial Revolution* (Yale University Press, 2012).

Ortutay, Barbara. "Social Design Site Quirky Launches US Made Product," *USA Today*, 13 June 2012.

Pappano, Laura. "The Year of the MOOC," *New York Times*, 12 November 2012.

Paul, Annie Murphy. "The Machines are Taking Over," *New York Times*, 14 September 2012.

PBS. "Nova Science Now: What are Animals Thinking?," 8 November 2012.

Perry, Douglas. "IBM Says Practical Quantum Computers are Close," http://www.hardware.com/ibm-qubit-super-computers, 14832.html.

Rainie, Lee and Wellman, Barry. *Networked, the New Social Operating System* (The MIT Press, 2012).

Rich, Sarah and Madrigal, Alex. "A Tiny Balloon Factory, Small-Batch Whiskey, and 3D Printing: A Dispatch from the Future of Manufacturing," *The Atlantic*, 26 September 2012.

Rosin, Hanna. *The End of Men* (Riverside Books, 2012).

Rusli, Evelyn M. and Wingfield, Nick. "Microsoft Buys Business Only Social Network," *New York Times*, 30 November 2012.

S-W, C. "Nothing to Fear: Apps for Tracking Workers' Productivity," *The Economist*, 14 October 2013.

Salter, Chuck. "The Doctor of the Future," *Fast Company*, 1 May 2009.

Saylor, Michael. *The Mobile Wave: How Mobile Intelligence Will Change Everything* (Persell Books/Vanguard Press, 2012).

Seligson, Hannah. "University Consortium to Offer Small Online Courses for Credit," *New York Times*, 15 November 2012.

Stills, Stephen. "For What It's Worth," 1967, ATCO.

Talwar, Rohit and Hancock, Tim. "The Shape of Jobs to Come, Possible New Careers Emerging from Advances in Science and Technology (2010-2030)", UK Department for Business Innovation and Skills, January 2010.

Techterms.com "Server."

The Web Chronology Project. "The Industrial Revolution," www.thenagain.inso/webchron/westeurope/indrew.html.

TimeToast. "Agricultural Revolution," www.timetoast.com/timelines/agricultural-revolution-.2.

Topol, Eric. *The Creative Destruction of Medicine* (Basic Books, 2011).

Turkle, Sherry. *Alone Together: Why We Expect More From Technology and Less From Each Other* (Basic Books, 2011).

"Disruptions: Texting Your Feelings Symbol by Symbol," *New York Times*, 18 August 2013.

Victorian Web. "The Victorian Web," www.victorianweb.org/technology/ir/ichron.html.

Wagner, Kurt. "70% of Fortune 500 CEOs do not use any social networks," August 7 2013, http://mashable.com/2013/08/07/fortune-500-ceos-social-media/.

Wallace, Shawn. "Maker Faire New York," *MAKE*, 26 September 2012.

Wikipedia: "3D Printing"; "Industrial Revolution" ; "Productivity Improving Technologies (Historical)"; "Productivity"; "Quantum Computer"; "Time Table of Agricultural and Food Technology."

Williams, Alex. "The Emily Posts of the Digital Age," *New York Times*, 29 March 2013.

"Working Alone. Together," *New York Times*, 13 May 2013.

Wingfield, Nick. "Despite a Slowdown, Smartphone Advances Are Still Ahead," *New York Times*, 16 September 2012.

World Future Society. "Wright's Law: A Better Predictor of Technological Progress than Moore's Law," *World Future Society*, Vol. 13, No. 9, September 2012.

The Book Cover

Croatian designer Gordon Blazevic created a cover that represents the theme of the book. The seemingly random text underneath the book title is not really random, but rather is a Latin text called Lorem Ipsum. It is generally used in graphic design to represent any text, so in a way it is seen as a pure text itself. In this case, it is made more generic by stripping it of any punctuation. Another layer of meaning is in font choices, with a centuries old font used for book printing far before modern digital technologies, and a second contemporary font that was created for the purpose of new digital technologies. In a subtle way, this suggests the process by which new technologies converge to change reality. Another layer of meaning is in the background illustration, which is actually a stretched lithograph from the 15th century showing Gutenberg's printing press and people working on it. Printing is a job that is now done in a completely different way as a result of new digital technologies, but it is basically still the same job. Of course, Gutenberg's invention of the printing press is considered by many to be the beginning of what we consider the modern era of technology.

About the Author

Richard Lieberman is the best-selling author of *Personal Foul: Coach Joe Moore vs. The University of Notre Dame* (Academy Chicago, 2001). He is a partner with the international law firm of McGuireWoods, where he specializes in employment and intellectual property law.

He can be contacted at Ricklieber@gmail.com and on Twitter as @RickLieberman1.